MW00358878

# PIONEERS

## IN

# PARADISE

# PIONEERS IN PARADISE

## West Palm Beach ~ The First 100 Years

JAN TUCKWOOD & ELIOT KLEINBERG
*The Palm Beach Post*

LP
LYONS PRESS

Guilford, Connecticut

An imprint of The Rowman & Littlefield Publishing Group, Inc.
4501 Forbes Blvd., Ste. 200
Lanham, MD 20706
www.rowman.com

Distributed by NATIONAL BOOK NETWORK

Copyright © 1994 The Palm Beach Post
First Lyons Press edition 2019

On page 2: Phillips Point office tower in West Palm Beach and the Society of the Four Arts pyramid in Palm Beach.

*All rights reserved.* No part of this book may be reproduced in any form or by any electronic or mechanical means, including information storage and retrieval systems, without written permission from the publisher, except by a reviewer who may quote passages in a review.

British Library Cataloguing in Publication Information available

**Library of Congress Cataloging-in-Publication Data available**

ISBN 978-1-4930-4222-7 (paperback)

∞™ The paper used in this publication meets the minimum requirements of American National Standard for Information Sciences—Permanence of Paper for Printed Library Materials, ANSI/NISO Z39.48-1992.

# Contents

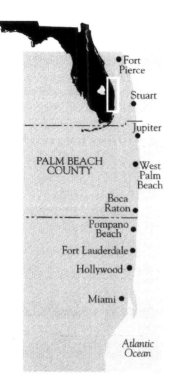

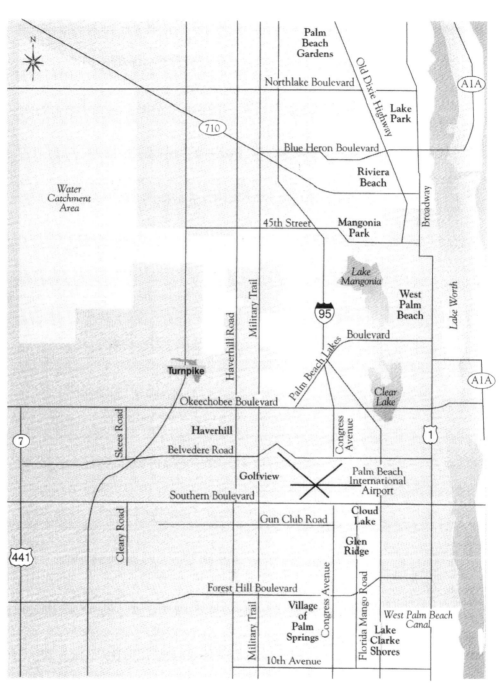

WEST PALM
BEACH,
FLORIDA, 1994
*The city limits,
shown in yellow, are
a far cry from the
original city plan laid
out by Henry Flagler
in 1893.* ■

# Introduction

*by Edward M. Sears*
*Editor*, The Palm Beach Post

There was always the land, the water and the mosquitoes. Our pioneers added the vital and the trivial; the bridges and the bulkheads; the schools and the cisterns; the pineapples and the coconuts; the governments and the politics; the houses of worship and the grounds for the dead. And much, much more. Somehow, mostly with luck and love, they left us with matters in a reasonable enough state to plow ahead into a second hundred years.

Oh, there are plenty of stories that challenge us to set things right during our watch. In researching this book, we learned of stately buildings that were replaced by parking lots. Once you could flip a quarter off the Southern Boulevard bridge and watch it spin lazily to the bottom of Lake Worth. Not too long ago the beaches hadn't given way to the usually tacky and occasionally magnificent monuments that await final judgment from a class five hurricane.

Much of this transition from swamp to city is found in the pages of *The Palm Beach Post*. Nothing is more grounded in a community than its newspaper, which records both good and foul deeds and creates an institutional memory for all time.

While rummaging through *The Post's* past, I discovered some lively predecessors. Big Joe Earman, for instance, not only recorded history, he made it while carrying on a long-distance feud with the governor, Sidney Catts. Here are highlights from a memorable 1920 letter the governor wrote to Big Joe:

Dear Sir:

I received a copy of your *Palm Beach Post* with your page and a half of vituperations and bitterness against me . . . Now I have got to speak plainly with you . . . If you print one more page in your paper like this last one . . . I will go to West Palm Beach, Florida, with my double-barrel shotgun loaded with buckshot and I will have a final settlement with you. You say your printer's ink is worth 10 cents a drop, but I say 14 buckshots in each gun barrel with a man who will pull the trigger weighs one thousand pounds each . . . This is a last warning and all that I have to say.

*Yours very truly, Sidney J. Catts*

Looking over my daily mail, it's comforting to know that time doesn't change some things. Perhaps 100 years from now, in the book celebrating our second century, one or two of my more notable letters will be included among the tributes to the land, the water and the mosquitoes.

*MORRISON FIELD, 1952*
Post *editor Edward M. Sears with his sister, Judy, and his father, Edward M. Sears Sr., an Air Force captain stationed here before being sent to Korea. The children attended Northboro Elementary during the year-long stay and eventually settled 40 miles farther south. In 1985, Sears returned to edit* The Post. ■

## JUPITER LIGHTHOUSE, 1891

*The Jupiter Lighthouse first lit up the shallow waters off the Jupiter Inlet in 1860. Gen. George Meade, who would later win the battle of Gettysburg, designed the light to guide mariners over the treacherous shallows. During the Civil War, Confederate blockade-runners familiar with the waters didn't need the light and didn't want it revealing them to Union patrols. Assistant keeper August Oswald Lang, a German immigrant now a proud citizen of the Confederate States of America, ordered his boss to surrender the lighting mechanism. J.F. Papy, loyal to his federal paycheck, said no, but was convinced otherwise. The rebels hid the light, and it was recovered after the war. It was relighted in 1866 and, except for a brief outage during the great 1928 hurricane, has sent its beam sweeping 18 miles across the dark seas ever since.* ■

## Chapter 1

# Wilderness & War

## 1513-1873

West Palm Beach's story cannot be told without its real beginning — the early days of Florida itself.

Florida's history is rich with tales of Indians, Spanish conquerors, British loyalists — and a natural wilderness so treacherous and unknown that white settlers didn't begin to tame its southern half until 1860, when Jupiter became the first settlement in what is now Palm Beach County.

Before 1513 and the arrival of Ponce de León, hundreds of thousands of Indians lived in what would become Florida. The Jeaga and Ais tribes laid claim to what is now the Gold and Treasure coasts.

Two hundred years later, they were gone: some slain by each other and the white invaders, most killed by European diseases. Then came the Seminoles and Miccosukees, who migrated from the present Alabama and Georgia.

The Spaniards called this land *La Florida*, and it eventually sprawled from near New Orleans on the west to the mysterious Everglades. Their flag flew for two-and-a-half centuries. Spain briefly lost *La Florida* to England, regained it, then gave it up for good to the fledgling United States in 1821.

America picked up where the Conquistadors left off. Three wars forced the Seminoles and Miccosukees out of Florida or deep into the Everglades. Then, the Civil War tore America apart and Florida left the Union, only to return in the humiliation of defeat and occupation.

Soon after the war, pioneers began the journey to the endless scrub and sand of South Florida.

Some of them, like Marion Dimick Geer's family, settled along a body of water the Indians had called "Hypoluxo" — "water all around, can't get out." By the time the Geers arrived in 1876, the closed-in lagoon and the surrounding region were called "Lake Worth." There, Marion Geer wrote in 1896, those pioneers found a "Garden of Eden" — and tamed the last frontier in the Eastern United States.

*PONCE DE LEÓN*
*Indians had been living in Florida for thousands of years by the time the Spanish explorer discovered the state in 1513. The first detailed account of South Florida was in 1696, when Jonathan Dickinson was shipwrecked off Jupiter.* ■

# Key events, 1513 - 1873

*Florida in 1763*

*Florida in 1833*

**April 1513:** Juan Ponce de León explores Florida coast and claims it for Spain.

**Sept. 8, 1565:** Pedro Menéndez de Avilés founds St. Augustine. *La Florida* officially under Spanish rule.

**Dec. 13, 1566:** Fort Santa Lucia established at Jupiter Inlet. It is soon abandoned.

**Sept. 23, 1696:** Shipwreck strands Quaker Jonathan Dickinson and his family near Jupiter Island. Journal of his two-month walk to St. Augustine is the first detailed account of region.

**1565-1700s:** Spanish expand settlements and build more than 130 missions. Original Indian tribes — whose population was estimated at 300,000 in Florida before the 1500s — are wiped out by massacres, battles, slave trade and European diseases.

**Feb. 10, 1763:** Spain trades Florida to England for Cuba. British split *La Florida* along Apalachicola River, creating colonies of East and West Florida.

**1776-1783:** British Floridas stay loyal to England in U.S. Revolution.

**April 21, 1783:** England, smarting from U.S. Revolution loss, returns Floridas to Spain for the Spanish-seized Bahamas.

**1795:** Spain creates Florida's current boundaries.

**1700s-1800s:** Seminole Indians migrate into North Florida from southern U.S.

**1818:** First Seminole War; Gen. Andrew Jackson chases Seminoles through Spanish Florida.

**Feb. 22, 1821:** Spain sells Florida to U.S. for $5 million.

**Dec. 29, 1824:** Mosquito County, which includes present-day Palm Beach County, formed.

**1830:** First U.S. census in Florida sets population at 34,730. South Florida: 517.

**1835-1842:** Second Seminole War.

**Feb. 4, 1836:** Dade County created; it covers 6,000 square miles from upper Keys north to Hillsboro River (Deerfield Beach/Boca Raton) and the south shore of Lake Okeechobee. Indian Key made county seat.

**Dec. 25, 1837:** Battle of Okeechobee, largest and last great clash of the war.

**1838:** Tennessee Volunteers carve supply trail through what will become Palm Beach County — the future Military Trail.

**January 1838:** Battles of Jupiter and Lockahatchee (Loxahatchee). Fort Jupiter established.

**1840:** Population: Florida 54,477.

**1840-1842:** Soldiers discover and name Lake Worth, in honor of William Jenkins Worth, leader of U.S. forces in Second Seminole War.

**1842:** At least 21 men apply to settle lake area under Armed Occupation Act, which gave each settler 160 acres. Group gone by early 1870s.

**March 9, 1844:** Dade County seat moved from Indian Key to Miami.

**March 3, 1845:** Florida admitted to the Union as 27th state.

**1850:** Population: Florida 87,445.

**1853-1856:** Third Seminole War, last Indian war east of Mississippi.

**1855-1866:** Dade County expands north to the St. Lucie Inlet (Stuart), including what is now Palm Beach County.

*Florida counties in 1840*

**Aug. 13, 1855:** Region's first post office opens at Fort Jupiter. It closes Feb. 26, 1856.

**1860:** Population: Florida 140,424 (45 percent black).

**July 10, 1860:** Jupiter Lighthouse begins operation. First families settle around lighthouse.

**1861-1865:** Civil War devastates Florida. State sends 15,000 soldiers; one-third die. State suffers second-largest economic decline of Confederate states.

**Jan. 10, 1861:** Florida secedes from United States.

*August Lang*

**April 15, 1861:** August Lang, assistant keeper of Jupiter lighthouse, seizes lighting mechanism to help Confederate blockade runners. He hides it until after war.

**April 22, 1861:** Florida joins Confederate States of America.

**June 28, 1866:** Jupiter lighthouse relighted.

**1870:** Population: Florida 187,748, Dade County 85.

## MILES AND MILES OF NOTHING

*This 1885 photograph shows pioneers standing on what is believed to be the west side of Lake Worth — the future West Palm Beach. Clear Lake is in the background. George Potter is at left, his brother, Dr. Richard Potter (the area's first physician) is third from right. The woman next to George is probably Ellen Potter, the Potter brothers' sister, who owned many acres of land near Clear Lake. The woman in the white dress and the child are unidentified, and the identities of the other men are speculation, but they are believed to be George Lainhart (fifth from left), H.F. Hammon (second from right) and Will Lanehart (right).*

## Chapter 2

# Frontier Days

## 1873-1893

**W**hat lured the pioneers here? Why did they spend harrowing days and nights, sailing and poling through narrows and swamps, to get to an insect-infested wilderness called Lake Worth?

Simple: True grit and true beauty.

As Captain Bravo, who sailed a steamer from Sebastian to Jupiter in the late 1880s would tell visitors, "See Lake Worth and die happy!"

So, the pioneers came. And they paid a high price for the clear water and lush greenery of Lake Worth: Mosquitoes thick enough to kill cows, wildcats that ate their chickens, hurricanes that would strike without warning, no doctors, no mail, no schools. They were like Robinson Crusoe — practically cut off from the world.

These pioneers called the area from Jupiter to Hypoluxo the "Lake Worth region," and they traveled from one homestead to another by boat. H.F. Hammon was the first to file a homestead claim on what is now Palm Beach. H.D. Pierce was second to file a claim; he settled on Hypoluxo Island.

The most influential settler in the early years was E.N. "Cap" Dimick, who got his nickname because he favored white caps, not because he was a sailor. ("He was not a captain of any size ship!" his grandson, T.T. Reese Jr., says.) Dimick became the first hotelier in Palm Beach and the first mayor, and was elected to the state senate.

His extended family settled on Palm Beach in 1876, and his descendants remain in the area. So do the descendants of L.W. Burkhardt, George Lainhart, George Potter and other pioneers.

It must have been incredible to them when, 20 years after they arrived, their wilderness became one of the most highfalutin resorts in all the world — Palm Beach.

*THE FIRST HOMES*
*Ben Lanehart, holding a rifle in front of his "palmetto shack" on the west side of Lake Worth, in what would become West Palm Beach, around 1885. Lanehart was a second cousin of brothers Will Lanehart and George Lainhart (they spelled their names differently), who would become prominent in West Palm Beach. His shack is typical of early pioneer homes. "When new, these shacks are pleasant shelters with the fresh odor of the newly cut leaves and are rather pretty, light green in color and clean," pioneer Lillie Pierce Voss wrote in a memoir, "but an old one is brown, leaky and full of roaches; very frequently a house snake lives in the roof to catch roaches."* ■

# Key events: 1873-1893

Cocoanut Grove House

The first hotel, Cap Dimick's Cocoanut Grove House, shown here in a sketch by George Potter. The hotel burned in 1893. ■

**July 28, 1873:** First formal homestead claim in Lake Worth region filed by H.F. Hammon, an Ohioan. Second homestead claim filed shortly after by Hannibal Pierce, father of Charles Pierce, one of the barefoot mailmen and author of *Pioneer Life in Southeast Florida.* "Lake region" population less than a dozen.

**1875:** Federal government builds Gilbert's Bar House of Refuge on Hutchinson Island, one of nine on Florida coast, including Orange Grove house in Delray Beach.

**1876:** Storm, possibly a hurricane, levels fledgling settlement.

**Jan. 9, 1878:** Providencia wrecks in Palm Beach with 20,000 coconuts;

proliferation of coconut palm trees leads to town's name.

**1880:** Population: Florida 269,493; Dade County 257. Around this time, E.N. "Cap" Dimick opens first hotel, the Cocoanut Grove House.

**May 21, 1880:** Lake Worth region post office established.

**September 1880:** Irving R. Henry, believed to be first home-steader on west side of lake, files claim for 131 acres. Henry later sells property, at point where Datura meets the lake — later 213 Narcissus St. — to O.S. Porter.

**1881:** Region gets first doctor, Richard Potter.

**1884:** The Rev. Elbridge Gale builds first log cabin on west side of lake.

**1885:** "Barefoot mailman" route established from Jupiter Lighthouse to Cape Florida (Key Biscayne)

**March 1886:** Dade County's first schoolhouse opens in Palm Beach. Rev. Gale's daughter, Hattie, is the teacher.

**Jan. 15, 1887:** Post office established for Palm City. Renamed Oct. 1 as Palm Beach.

**Oct. 10, 1887:** Barefoot mailman Ed Hamilton lost crossing Hillsboro Inlet, drowned or killed by sharks or alligators.

**1888:** Caloosahatchee Canal completed, connecting Gulf coast with Lake Okeechobee.

**Jan 5, 1889:** First church, Bethesda-by-the-Sea, opens in schoolhouse. First church building opens in April.

**Feb. 18, 1889:** County seat moves from Miami to Juno.

**July 4, 1889:** Jupiter and Lake Worth (Celestial) Railway, first in South Florida, opens, spanning 7 1/2 miles from Jupiter to Juno.

**1890:** Population: Florida 391,422, Dade County 995.

**December 1892:** First road to Biscayne Bay region opens from Lantana to North Miami.

**1893:** Henry Flagler visits Palm Beach and buys lakefront and ocean-front land for $125,000 and O.S. Porter and Louis Hillhouse family property on west side for $45,000.

*Florida counties in 1880*

*Bethesda-by-the-Sea Episcopal Church was founded in 1889. This building, the church's second, was built in 1894.* ∎

"OURS WAS IN A MEASURE AN IDEAL EXISTENCE" *George W. Potter sketched this pioneer woman and Seminole Indian, walking on the western side of Lake Worth — the future West Palm Beach. The first Bethesda-by-the-Sea Church, built in 1889, is behind them in Palm Beach.* ■

# We Pioneers

## How we lived off the bounty of the land and sea and "made the wilderness to blossom"

*by Marion Dimick Geer*
*The Lake Worth Historian, 1896*

Marion Geer and her family left their home on an Illinois farm in December 1875 and came south, "determined to colonize and seek that flowery land where Ponce de León so faithfully sought the fabled spring of eternal youth."

Her party included her husband Albert and his two sisters, her parents, and her brothers (E.N. Dimick, known as "Cap," and F.L. Dimick).

The three Dimick children had married the three Geer children. Marion, who was called "Pink" because of her rosy complexion, wrote a memoir for *The Lake Worth Historian* in 1896, detailing the hardships of the pioneer families in Lake Worth. This is an edited excerpt.

As our desire was to locate in a place below frost line where tropical fruits could be safely cultivated, a commodious house was rented at Jacksonville where the three families could be made comfortable while the men went on a prospecting tour.

They sought long and diligently for one spot in all Florida more abundantly blessed with climate, productive soil and convenient transportation than any other. After months of wandering they returned, declaring with one accord that at Lake Worth, 300 miles south, they had found a veritable "Garden of Eden," where the sky was bluer, the water clearer, the flowers sweeter, the song of birds more musical than could be found elsewhere on the continent.

Could mortal woman ask more, unreasonable as the sages declare her to be? We did not, and in September 1876, thitherward we turned our faces.

On the evening of the second day's sailing and poling through narrows and over oyster beds, we reached Jupiter, where we were kindly received by the superintendent of the lighthouse. Next morning a small boat was procured and we were set down in our "Garden of Eden."

Oh, desolation! What a place to travel weary days and nights to find!

There seemed absolutely nothing to build our hopes upon, surely not the thin soil with the coquina rock cropping out everywhere.

What could we have done in our discouragement without the courage

*"YOUNG TIGER"*
*The Seminoles and the pioneers lived harmoniously. George Potter's sketch of "Young Tiger" was made in 1874 near Miami.* ■

# Lake Country Pioneers

*As listed by the Lake Worth Pioneers Association.*

"Cap" Dimick was Palm Beach's first hotelier, first mayor and a state senator.

Will Lanehart, brother of George Lainhart (they spelled their names differently), and H.F. Hammon, the lake region's first homesteader, around 1920.

George W. Lainhart, co-founder of Lainhart & Potter lumber company and a Dade County commissioner.

## 1873-1886

H.F. Hammon
H.D. Pierce
W.M. Lanehart
E.N. Dimick
A. Geer
D. Brown
M.E. Spencer
B. Lanehart
U.D. Hendrickson
E.M. Brelsford
G. Charters
J.C. Hoagland
A.E. Heyser
G.W. Lainhart
R.B. Potter
J.W. Davidson
J.P. McKenna
E. Gale
A.W. Garnett
R.R. McCormick
G.S. Rowley
W.H. Moore
C. Moore
H.P. Dye
M.W. Dimick
F.L. Dimick
V.O. Spencer
E.R. Bradley
A. Wilder
J. McFarland
J.H. Brelsford
F. Lennon
I. Henry

C.A. Lane
G.W. Potter
R.B. Moore
C.C. Haight
C.I. Cragin
G. Gale
J.W. Porter
O.S. Porter
J.J. White

## 1886-1893

N.W. Pitts
L.D. Hillhouse
J.T. Earnest
J.N. Parker
J.W. Comstock
F.S. Dewey
M.B. Lyman
C.V. Barton
J.W. Clark
H.C. Hood
F. Robert
J.W. Mulligan
H. Sanders
D. Burnett
G. Sears
A. Nelson
C.J. Clarke
L.W. Burkhardt
S.F. Worthington
J.W. Perry
H.M. Flagler
A. Fields
D.A. Allen
F. Kinzel
W. Whidden
R.K. Brown
F.C. Voss
J.J. Haley
J.H. Dick
H.J. Burkhardt
E. Root

and steadfast faith of our parents, who, with their early experience of pioneer life in Michigan, put new hope in our fainting hearts and fired us with zeal?

A place was quickly cleared for our first house, which was completed in three weeks. A hurricane, soon after our arrival, scattered our goods hither and yon — table, stove, chairs and bureau were blown about and dropped far and near, which was not in accordance with our ideas of the gentle zephyrs we had been told fanned the cheeks of those who lived in this favored region.

Being anxious that Lake Worth should, as soon as possible, take on the appearance of a flourishing settlement, as well as for our own convenience, we planned at this time to build two more houses. A large boat was chartered in which the building material could be brought from Jacksonville. With the load were shipped chickens and a mule.

To be sure there were many things connected with this pioneer life hard to endure. With St. Lucie the nearest post office, 65 miles north, and Miami 75 miles south, with no carrier between, and our grocery and dry goods stores at Titusville, 130 miles away, our mail came by whomsoever chanced to be coming our way. The news of President Garfield's death came in a paper thrown by a passing steamer to one of our boats.

But no steamer could throw us a can of kerosene, baking powder or other housekeeping necessities. They came, though, most bountifully, and we grew to depend upon the ocean as our carrier, looking upon that restless body as the servant of Him whose promise to provide we had not doubted.

Sometimes the generosity of the waves appalled us; we needed lard and seven barrels came, 2,800 pounds! We needed kerosene and cans of it were washed ashore. Along with it came boxes of bacon and tobacco, and cans of turpentine and varnish.

In one hurricane which swept the coast before our arrival, Mr.

*POTTER HOME, 1893 George Potter moved to the west side of the lake in 1893 and built this house for his young wife, Ella Dimick Potter.* ■

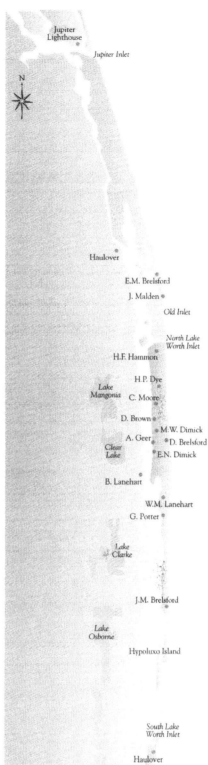

*LAKE WORTH REGION And the homesteads of its pioneers, 1883, from Pioneer Life in Southeast Florida by Charles Pierce.* ■

Jupiter Lighthouse

Jupiter Inlet

N

Haulover

E.M. Brelsford

J. Malden

Old Inlet

North Lake Worth Inlet

H.F. Hammon

H.P. Dye

Lake Mangonia

C. Moore

D. Brown

M.W. Dimick

A. Geer

D. Brelsford

Clear Lake

E.N. Dimick

B. Lanehart

W.M. Lanehart

G. Potter

Lake Clarke

J.M. Brelsford

Lake Osborne

Hypoluxo Island

South Lake Worth Inlet

Haulover

## A PALM BEACH PICNIC, AROUND 1885

*Picnics were popular entertainment for the pioneers. This group dines on the shore of Lake Worth (the tower in the background was probably a lookout for shipwrecks). George Potter is at right and his brother, Dr. Richard Potter, is second from left. It is believed that the woman in the plaid dress is their sister, Ellen Potter, and the man at left is H.F. Hammon. The child and the other woman are unidentified.* ■

Charlie Moore told us everything from pins and needles to a saw mill came, including a large amount of money and a fine cook stove (in spite of the fact that iron will sink). Trunks containing ladies' clothing, too — and Mr. Moore assured us he wore trimmed underclothes for some time, having no wife to utilize them.

Ours was in a measure an ideal existence, for selfishness was not one of its elements. Our joys and sorrows, our misfortunes and successes, were general, not individual. For even in this, our "Eden," sorrow and misfortune came.

We had no laws against poaching, and although "welcome" did not hang from the trees and was not written upon the hunting ground, it was in our hearts, and shone from our faces, I am sure, so glad were we to share our abundance with others.

Some of the hunters who came to our preserve were accustomed to set guns for deer, by attaching a string to the trigger and waiting till the animal should run upon it. One night a gun had been set and the men were keeping watch from a palmetto shanty, but unfortunately fell asleep. The son of one of our neighbors, who was out torch hunting, received the charge in his leg.

We had no physician and but limited knowledge for such a case, and after much suffering, he died — the first visit of the dark-robed death angel to our colony.

We had no minister and no undertaker, but were able to make a casket, and with a few verses from the Book, which here as elsewhere was our staff, and a sweet hymn, we laid him to rest in his father's dooryard.

In January 1878, a vessel loaded with coconuts and logwood (the Providencia) was wrecked off our coast and about 20,000 nuts secured, distributed, and planted, thus enabling each settler to have as large a grove as he pleased.

Mr. Geer, who owned and improved the land where the Royal Poinciana now stands, planted 900 nuts which, with 600 other tropical trees comprising 26 varieties, made a place we had earned the right to be proud of; earned it by days, months and years of labor, such as pioneers alone can know.

And when, upon the arrival of R.R. McCormick, he exclaimed with evident surprise: "Truly this is a paradise, you have made the wilderness to blossom," we were gratified.

In 1886, the Geers sold their land to R.R. McCormick of Denver for $10,000 and moved back north to a Michigan farm. Seven years later, McCormick sold it to Henry Flagler for $75,000. Here, Flagler built his first and largest Palm Beach hotel, the Royal Poinciana.

## THE PROVIDENCIA

*On Jan. 9, 1878, the 175-ton brig Providencia, headed from the Caribbean to Spain, wound up on the beach. Pioneers H.F. Hammon and Will Lanehart confronted the captain, and Lanehart later wrote: "I was greeted by the mate of the vessel, with a bottle of wine and a box of cigars, as a sort of olive branch. There were 20,000 coconuts, and they seemed like a God-send to the people. For several weeks, everyone was eating coconuts and drinking wine."*

*Lanehart and Hammon sold the nuts for 2 1/2 cents each. By 1885, when the photo on the next pages was taken, the island was lush with coconut palms. Dr. Richard Potter is the first man on the left, the woman at right is believed to be his sister, Ellen. The others are unidentified, but the man sitting in the center could be H.F. Hammon.* ∎

## Pioneer Profile

# George W. Potter & Richard Potter
## 1851-1924           1845-1909

*by David Willson*
*Great-grandson of George W. Potter*

*POTTER LEGACY*
*David Willson, 42, is an artist, like his great-grandfather, George Potter, portrayed in the bust. Opposite page: Family treasures, including a jar that washed up with the coconuts of the Providencia in 1878, Potter's diary, his 1896 drawing of his wife, Ella, and a 1901 photo of his daughter, Marjorie, who died in 1990 at age 92.* ■

Richard and George Potter left Cincinnati in the bitter cold December of 1873, bound for Florida. It was a trip born of necessity — George was asthmatic, and his older brother Richard, a doctor, decided warm weather would restore his health.

They headed first to Lemon City, now north Miami. But in 1881, they moved north. George settled on Palm Beach, about a mile south of where Southern Boulevard is today. Richard followed, as did their mother, Lydia, their sister, Ellen, and their adopted brother, Bernard. George's homestead, "Figulus," spanned 160 acres from ocean to lake.

In 1893, he sold his property — part of it to the owner of the Tutti-Frutti gum company and part to Richard Croker, the notorious Tammany Hall chief — and moved across the lake to build a home for his bride, Ella Dimick, niece of Cap Dimick. Then he launched a series of important "firsts" in West Palm Beach:

■ He and George Lainhart started the first lumber company, Lainhart & Potter.

■ He formed the first real-estate firm, Porter & Potter, with Capt. O.S. Porter.

■ He surveyed much of West Palm Beach. Potter Road is named for him, and Ellamar Road is named for his wife, Ella, and their daughter, Marjorie.

He was also a city alderman and mayor. But perhaps George Potter's most lasting gift is his art: sketches of early West Palm Beach and its people.

Richard's gift was medicine — he was the Lake Worth area's first doctor. Midwife Millie Gildersleeve, a freed slave from Georgia, assisted him. When it was time for a pioneer baby to be born, Richard would bring his motor launch up to Millie's wharf, toot his whistle, and Millie would scurry out with her instruments.

Millie raised five children of her own and died in 1950 at 88. Many of her descendants — and the descendants of the babies they delivered — still live in West Palm Beach.

# The firsts

## The first mailmen:
## Barefoot and brave

In the 1880s, with no railroad or regular ship service, a letter from Miami to Jupiter would make a six- to eight-week odyssey via Key West, Havana and New York.

So between 1885 and 1893, 11 rugged pioneers traversed the 136 miles, 56 in small boats and 80 on foot, between Palm Beach and Cape Florida, at the tip of Key Biscayne. The grueling trip took three days each way. They walked barefoot at the edge of the surf, where sand was hardest.

One of the 11, James E. "Ed" Hamilton, never completed his appointed round. On Oct. 9, 1887, at the Hillsboro Inlet, near Pompano Beach, he saw someone had stolen his boat. In stormy seas, he tried to swim the cove.

The next day, mail contractor George Charter and others went looking for Hamilton. They found only his bag, and Charter concluded he was drowned, or worse.

"The first thing he said was, 'Hamilton's gone. Sharks got him,' " fellow barefoot mailman Charles W. Pierce recounted in his memoir, *Pioneer Life in Southeast Florida.* Pierce surmises alligators were to blame.

A new road to Miami in 1892 spelled the end of the barefoot mailman. The popular 1943 novel by Theodore Pratt, *The Barefoot Mailman,* was based on the lives of Hamilton and Pierce.

## Celestial Railroad:
## When Juno was the moon

The Celestial Railroad, first rail line in South Florida, was born on the Fourth of July 1889. Officially, it was the Jupiter and Lake Worth Railway, but it earned its romantic moniker five years later. From an oceanfront loading dock at Jupiter, it stretched diagonally 7 1/2 miles to the lake and the new Dade County seat, Juno. Intermediate stops were then cleverly named Venus and Mars.

The line ran on a 3-foot-wide narrow-gauge track. With no turnaround, it had to back up to Jupiter. Each trip took 30 minutes, and residents came to know the toot-toots of engineer Blus Rice's rendition of *Dixie*.

Ultimately, Henry Flagler and his rail empire crushed the Celestial. It stopped running in April 1895.

Three years later Miami wrested back the county seat, and soon after that, a fire consumed Juno. It would be a half-century before the nearby town of Juno Beach would resurrect the pioneer town's legacy.

*The Celestial Railroad was never larger than three freight cars, two passenger coaches and one steam engine — "Old No. 3." What it did have was engineer Blus Rice (center), who rode with his hounddog and even rented the dog out to riders who wanted to hunt along the route.* ■

## The first school: $200, elbow grease
## and a teenage teacher

In the mid-1880s, Ella Dimick and her fellow pioneer women decided it was time for their kids to go to school. But there wasn't a school in all of sprawling Dade County.

So, they convinced the county to give them $200 for materials for a 22-by-40-foot building. George Lainhart and other residents provided the elbow grease. The school went up about 1 mile north of where the Royal Poinciana Hotel was built in 1893.

Class started in early March 1886. Students sat at a long table built of scrap lumber, and chairs were bought with some of the $226.80 raised at a crafts sale.

Seven students, ranging from 6 to 17, were later joined by five more. Their education fell to a 16-year-old girl from Kansas who had never taught a day in her life: Hattie Gale.

A school was built in downtown West Palm Beach at Clematis Street and Poinsettia (now Dixie Highway), and the little schoolhouse closed in 1901. It was moved board by board to Phipps Ocean Park in 1960, rebuilt and reopened in 1990 for school history programs.

*Teacher Hattie Gale stands in the doorway of the first school, built in 1886. "There were lessons learned by all, and some were not in books," she would recall a decade later. "When the term closed, both pupils and teacher knew that something had been accomplished."* ■

PALM BEACH'S GRANDEST DAME, THE ROYAL POINCIANA
*Nothing represented the dramatic change in Palm Beach more than Flagler's Royal Poinciana Hotel, which opened in mid-February 1894. A month later, Flagler's railroad reached West Palm Beach, opening it to the world.* ■

## Chapter 3

# The Flagler Era
## 1893-1913

*A stretch of the whitest of white sand, two lines of steel rails, a few acres of pineapples, a couple of houses, and "scrub" on every side! This was West Palm Beach in September, 1894.*

— Gula E. White
*The Lake Worth Historian, 1896*

By 1893, pioneer life around Lake Worth was all but over. Henry Flagler had opened up the frontier — and fast.

The Standard Oil tycoon, who had already turned St. Augustine into a winter resort, had come to Palm Beach in 1893 and declared it a "veritable paradise." He was sold by those beautiful coconut palms, planted by the pioneers.

Then he began buying land — paying $75,000 for the old Geer home in Palm Beach, which was then owned by R.R. McCormick of Denver, and $50,000 for a piece of E.M. Brelsford's land. Soon, the massive Royal Poinciana Hotel would rise on McCormick's land and Flagler's marble palace, Whitehall, would be built on Brelsford's. Across the lake, he bought a strip of land that stretched from Lake Worth to Clear Lake, paying $35,000 for Captain O.S. Porter's homestead and $10,000 for Louie Hillhouse's land. That $45,000 investment became West Palm Beach, the city Flagler founded "for my help."

By now, South Florida's destiny was clear: Land was the hot commodity, and nearly everyone in town was trying to buy and sell it.

In 1894, Flagler's railroad arrived, luring newcomers who dreamed of a bright future in a place of perpetual summer. Among them were the Anthony brothers, who launched a retailing empire on Clematis Street. And Joseph Jefferson, the actor, who brought electricity to the town. And Haley Mickens, who ran the "wheelchair" concession at E.R. Bradley's Beach Club.

Within the next 10 years, they would transform West Palm Beach from a servants' quarters into a real city.

*THE VISIONARY*
*Henry Flagler was an enigma — reserved in his private life but driven in business. In 1893, he created West Palm Beach and predicted, "In a few years, there'll be a town over there as big as Jacksonville."* ■

# Key events, 1893-1913

**May 1893:** Work begins on Royal Poinciana Hotel.

**May 11, 1893:** Dade County State Bank, first in region, established on Palm Beach.

**August 1893:** Henry Flagler lays out the 48-block town site of West Palm Beach.

**1894:** Fire destroys Juno. First building on Clematis Street opens as hardware store. Town's "dry" status lifted; whiskey comes to town, restricted to Banyan Street. Water plant built at Clear Lake.

**Feb. 4, 1894:** First West Palm Beach lots auctioned at Royal Poinciana Hotel.

**February 1894:** Flagler's grand Royal Poinciana Hotel opens in Palm Beach.

**March 22, 1894:** Flagler's Florida East Coast Railroad is completed to West Palm Beach.

**March 25, 1894:** Union Congregational Church, first church in West Palm Beach, founded at Datura and Olive.

**April 17, 1894:** West Palm Beach's first grocery store and post office opens.

**September 1894:** First school for blacks opens at Tabernacle Missionary Baptist Church, at Clematis and Tamarind.

*The "calaboose" (jailhouse) where West Palm Beach was incorporated.*

**Nov. 5, 1894:** West Palm Beach incorporated.

**Nov. 17, 1894:** "Flagler Alerts" volunteer fire department organized.

**1895:** City's first power plant begins operation.

**Nov. 16, 1895:** First bridge across lake, a railroad spur from around Banyan Street in downtown West Palm Beach, opens.

**January-February 1896:** Two fires devastate downtown business district.

**March 1896:** First train arrives at Royal Poinciana on special rail spur.

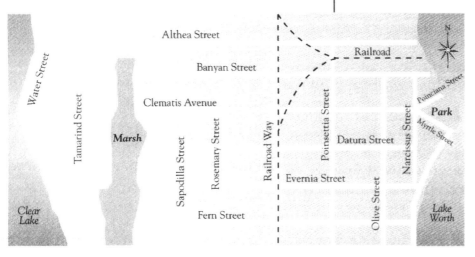

*West Palm Beach, as laid out by Henry Flagler in 1893.*

*Florida counties in 1900*

**April 21, 1896:** Railroad completed to Miami.

**May 10, 1899:** County seat returned to Miami from Juno.

**1900:** Population: Florida 528,542, Dade County 4,955, West Palm Beach 564.

**Nov. 25, 1900:** First library building opens in two-story lakefront building on Clematis Street.

**1901:** New rail and pedestrian bridge, at site of present Flagler Memorial Bridge, replaces earlier railroad spur, four blocks to the south.

**Sept. 1, 1902:** City fire department (a professional successor to the volunteer Flagler Alerts) organized.

**1903:** Town hall moves to upstairs of frame building at Datura and Poinsettia (Dixie).

**June 9, 1903:** The Breakers, Flagler's second Palm Beach hotel, burns.

**July 21, 1903:** West Palm Beach officially changes from a town to a city.

**Sept. 11, 1903:** Hurricane causes extensive damage to downtown area.

**1904:** The Breakers reopens.

**1905:** Telephone company set up; service established by 1907, with 18 phones connected.

*1911 telephone book*

**March 20, 1905:** Woodlawn Cemetery founded; it is deeded to the city in 1914.

**July 4, 1905:** City dedicates first permanent fire station.

**Oct. 28, 1908:** Carl Kettler opens Bijou, West Palm Beach's first theater, in Jefferson building along Clematis Street.

**1908:** Central school built on "the hill" at Hibiscus and Georgia streets, west of downtown. Site will later house Palm Beach High School.

**April 30, 1909:** Palm Beach County formed; West Palm Beach named as county seat. On July 6, courthouse opens at schoolhouse, Clematis and Poinsettia (Dixie).

**1910:** Population: Florida 752,619; Palm Beach County 5,577; West Palm Beach 1,743.

**1911:** Royal Park Bridge, a wooden trestle from Lakeview Avenue in West Palm Beach to Royal Palm Way in Palm Beach, opens. First airplane flies over area.

**April 17, 1911:** Palm Beach incorporated.

**Jan. 12, 1912:** Flagler opens railroad link to Key West.

**March 1912:** Palm Beach County Fair, forerunner to South Florida Fair, operates in a tent in downtown West Palm Beach.

**1913:** Town hall moves to second floor of fire station.

**May 20, 1913:** Flagler dies in Palm Beach.

*MARY LILY*

*By the time Flagler opened the Royal Poinciana in Palm Beach in 1894, his second wife, Ida Alice, was insane. In 1901, Flagler pushed a bill through the Florida Legislature allowing divorce on insanity grounds. This cleared the way for the 71-year-old Flagler to marry Mary Lily Kenan, 34. Mary Lily and the marble palace her husband built for her, Whitehall, became the toast of Palm Beach.* ■

# Who was Henry Flagler?

Henry Morrison Flagler's fortune started with a 5-cent piece, four pennies and a 5-franc coin he carried the rest of his life, a reminder of the lesson in a biblical parable: no risk, no gain.

He built one fortune, saw it collapse, and within five years was the second-in-command at Standard Oil and on his way to becoming one of America's wealthiest men.

He was private, aloof and vain: Even when he was nearly blind, he was never photographed wearing his glasses.

He was abundant in his charity but judged every penny spent or donated on how it would help his business.

The son of a minister, he was a man of strict morals who profited early in his career from the brokering of grain to whiskey makers. He closed his operations on Sundays but ignored the casino gambling going on under his nose.

He was an honorable man but spent $300 to buy his way out of the Civil War and helped Standard Oil build a reputation for ruthless monopoly.

His successes were tempered by personal tragedies. Of his three wives, he buried one and institutionalized another. He was estranged from his son for nearly two decades.

He made more money than he would ever need but still sought immortality.

So, at an age when most people retire, he began a second career that made him the pivotal person in Florida's modern history.

Before he was done, he had changed it forever.

## ELEGANCE AMID THE PALMS

*Henry Morrison Flagler, with friends at the Royal Poinciana Hotel around 1900. Flagler was born in 1830, spent his childhood in upstate New York, and then headed west to Ohio, where the family of his first wife, Mary Harkness, provided him with his first successes in their country store. Mary died in 1881 and Flagler married Ida Alice Shourds. They honeymooned in St. Augustine, where Flagler's Florida dream was born. He spent the last 20 years of his life in Florida.* ■

*Afternoon concert hour at the Royal Poinciana.*

*The Royal Poinciana as seen from the West Palm Beach docks.*

FLAGLER'S DOMAIN
*Left, the oceanfront Breakers hotel around 1920, with its beach casino. The sprawling Royal Poinciana and West Palm Beach are in the background. Below, a postcard showing the ballroom of the Royal Poinciana.* ■

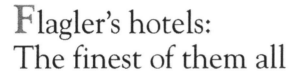

# Flagler's hotels: The finest of them all

How grand was the Royal Poinciana Hotel?

It took nine months and more than $1 million to build it, and as many as 20 of the 1,000 construction workers died in the process. But when it was done — in February 1894 — Palm Beach quickly became the mecca of "the 400," the cream of Gilded Age society.

The Royal Poinciana was the largest wooden structure in the world at the turn of the century — six stories high, plus two attic dormer floors, with 1,150 rooms and nearly 3 miles of corridors. Humorist Ring Lardner said the dining room was so vast (approximately two-thirds the size of a football field) that telephoning from one end to the other was a toll call.

Guests basked in luxury, riding around in "Afromobiles" powered by black employees, gathering for afternoon teas, and attending extravagant banquets and balls.

By March 1896, Flagler's railroad deposited guests at the hotel's door. And Flagler had opened another hotel — the small, oceanfront Palm Beach Inn. By 1901, he doubled its size and renamed it The Breakers.

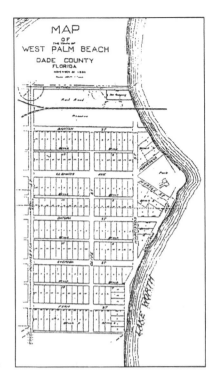

# Nov. 5, 1894: West Palm Beach is born

They gathered "atop the calaboose" (the jailhouse) at Poinsettia Avenue and Banyan Street — 87 people who wanted to legitimize their little town. They represented more than two-thirds of the potential voters, including some blacks. And they voted 77 to 1 to incorporate the city of West Palm Beach, establishing it from the Intracoastal Waterway west to Clear Lake and from Okeechobee Boulevard north to Bethesda Park, at about Seventh Street.

The first seal contained the words "West Palm Beach Florida. Incorporated Nov. 5, 1894," in a circle surrounding a cut coconut palm. Founders rejected the name "Flagler." The area had originally been called Westpalmbeach, a single-word, then split into three words.

In 1896, after three major storms hit and two fires damaged the downtown, numerologists blamed the fledgling city's woes on its name — it contained 13 letters.

*THE BEGINNING, 1893*

*This map of the core section of the city was made in November 1893. Streets were named in alphabetical order, after native plants. Running east and west were Althea, Banyan, Clematis, Datura, Evernia and Fern streets. North-south avenues were Lantana, Myrtle, Narcissus, Olive, Poinsettia (now Dixie Highway), Rosemary, Sapodilla and Tamarind.* ▪

*CELEBRATING THE FIRST BUILDING ON CLEMATIS, 1894*

*The first building on Clematis Street — a 12-by-20-foot hardware store run by Otto Weybrecht — went up in 1894. The Weybrecht family lived in the tent next door from 1893 until it was destroyed in the big Feb. 20, 1896, fire. Billy Bowlegs, the Seminole chief of that day, is in the foreground. Mrs. Weybrecht is the woman holding the baby, and the man second from left is the first dentist, Dr. J.A. Pugh.* ▪

# 1896 fires:
# The first disaster strikes

With most buildings made of wood, the water supply limited and a fire department still on the wish list, pioneer West Palm Beach was a giant fire hazard.

On Jan. 2, 1896, a 2 p.m. fire caused when a gasoline stove exploded struck at the town's central corner. It destroyed most of Banyan Street and a third of Narcissus Avenue. In all, a dozen stores and several offices were lost, including George Zapf's Seminole Hotel and the Dimick drug store.

Shaken city leaders passed the first fire code; all structures now had to be built of brick, brick veneer or stone.

But just weeks later, at 10 p.m. on Feb. 20, a second fire — a drunk tailor tipped an oil lamp — finished off much of the business district.

## Downtown Fires of 1896

**From a sketch by retailer A.P. Anthony.**
(Stores A through F were on the ground floor of The Palms Hotel, owned by J.C. Stowers, postmaster.)

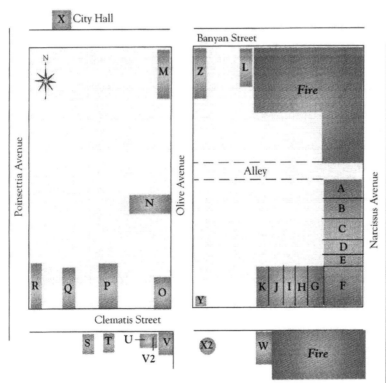

A. Ray and Day hardware
B. Anthony and Miller clothing and shoes (later absorbed by Anthony Bros.)
C. Post Office (Post Office occupied half; Anthony Bros. toys and fancy goods occupied half)
D. Vacant
E. Miss M.J. Ponce, millinery
F. Glen G. Strohm groceries
G. L.W. Burkhardt groceries
H. Capt. Chase, cold drinks
I. Mrs Knapp restaurant (specialty ham and eggs)
J. Conrad Schmidt's three-story wooden hotel
K. G.W. Idner and Son, jewelers
L. Will Whidden's meat market (where you could get any sized beef soup bone for five cents)
M. Lauther's saloon
N. Guy Metcalf's *Tropical Sun*
O. Dade County State Bank
P. Masonic Temple
Q. Edgar K. Pierce home
R. Al Haugh's bicycle shop
S. Mathis grocery store
T. Majewski's bakery
U. F.E.C. land offices
V. Bee Hive, cleaning and pressing establishment
V2. Lake Worth News
W. Weybrecht hardware
X. City Hall and Jail
X2. Where Cope the scavenger was located
Y. Lake Willson's shoe shop
Z. Row of small shops

AN IDYLLIC SETTING ON THE LAKE, 1900

*The lawn and lake were a playground for children of pioneer L.W. Burkhardt, whose home was at Fern Street and Lake Worth. Burkhardt came to the area from Philadelphia in 1893, just before the arrival of Henry Flagler. "Endowed with the hustling energy of the North and a prophetic vision of the future, he associated himself with his brother (H.J.*

Burkhardt, who had arrived several years earlier) and opened up a fruit and oyster business on the (Poinciana) hotel grounds," The Weekly Lake Worth News reported in 1900. The business was moved to West Palm Beach in 1894. L.W. Burkhardt became a town alderman, mayor and judge. Today, his descendants run Burkhardt Construction Inc. — and are key players in the 1994 redevelopment of downtown. ∎

# Joe Jefferson:
# A most electric soul

Next to Henry Flagler, the biggest spender in the development of early West Palm Beach was Joseph Jefferson, famed actor of the late 1800s.

Jefferson was as riveting as his friend Flagler was reserved. He put a spark into the new city — literally. He owned the first electric plant.

As one old-timer wrote in a memoir, Jefferson quoted from the Bible — "Let there be light!" — when he flipped on the electricity for the first time.

When a society matron confused him with "Alligator Joe," who had an alligator farm in Palm Beach, Jefferson replied, "Madame, I admit the Joe but deny the Alligator."

The actor also owned six houses, the Jefferson Hotel on Clematis Street, a two-story brick building on the southeast corner of Clematis and Olive that housed six stores, a store across the street that housed the Anthony Brothers retailers, and the first ice plant.

"His investments in the town must have amounted to $200,000 before he was through," wrote James Rembert Anthony, eldest of the Anthony brothers, in 1936. Anthony sat on the board of Jefferson's West Palm Beach companies and remembered the matinee-idol mogul this way:

"As an entertainer and actor, he was one of the greatest, but as a businessman, a 15-year-old boy could teach him. How he ever accumulated a fortune was always an enigma to us. A directors' meeting with him present was a riot. About the first thing brought up would remind him of a story — then all business was off for the rest of the afternoon and one laugh followed another."

*Joseph Jefferson, 1894*

### MATINEE IDOL AND MOGUL

*One of the most famous actors of the late 1800s was also one of early West Palm Beach's most important businessmen. Joseph Jefferson was even featured on postcards (left). Propelling his "Palm Beach coach" is his man Friday, Carl Kettler. Kettler's son, Carl Jr., would become well-known in West Palm Beach for opening the grand Bijou and Kettler theaters on Narcissus Street (see Chapter 4). The gold watch in the photo is inscribed to "Carl Kettler from Joseph Jefferson." The Masonic medal on the fob is Carl Kettler Jr.'s. The antique opera glasses are from that period, and the book, Joseph Jefferson, written in 1906, is open to show Jefferson in his most famous role: Rip Van Winkle. The actor died in Palm Beach on Easter Sunday, April 22, 1905. ∎*

## THE HEART OF THE BUSINESS DISTRICT: CLEMATIS AND NARCISSUS, EARLY 1900s

*This postcard shows Narcissus Avenue looking north from Clematis Street. The buildings at left — The Palms Hotel (foreground) and the Seminole Hotel — overlooked the City Park and Lake Worth. Note the "Post Office" sign. In the early days, mail delivery was a social event. As L.M. Currie, one of West Palm Beach's first teachers, wrote in 1922: "My thoughts naturally go back to the time of my arrival, just 26 years ago. The (train) station was then on Evernia Street, having been removed from its first location on the lake from Banyan Street, just a short time before. It seemed as if the entire population was at the station when I came, and I could not understand the reason, but I soon acquired the custom and with everyone else, participated in the main event of the day — meeting the evening train and going to the post office to wait for the distribution of mail. This custom interfered with social affairs, as no social gathering ever took place until after the arrival of the train. If the train was late, the party, boat ride, or whatever it might be, was later."* ■

*Clematis Street looking west. The Palms Hotel is at right.* ■

THE PEPPERS FAMILY IN THE STYX, AROUND 1906

*Thomas Peppers and his wife, Priscilla, with their four daughters. The children are, from left: Leaola, Ruth, Olethia and Inez. Inez Peppers Lovett is the only surviving member of her family.* ■

# Pioneer Profile

## Inez Peppers Lovett

Inez Peppers Lovett was born in 1895 near Tallahassee and was brought to Palm Beach when she was two months old. Her mother, Priscilla Robinson Peppers, had come with her aunt to work for Cap Dimick, Palm Beach's first hotelier. Her father, Thomas Peppers, from Georgia, was one of the first black men in Palm Beach. She provided these memoirs in the summer of 1994.

My grandparents were slaves. Grandfather buried the money he got while he was a slave and went back for it later. He saved the first dollar he ever got after slavery.

My father came here in the 1880s. We lived in the Styx, which was just shacks — no running water, no outside toilets, no electric lights. There was just one paved street, from the lake to the ocean, and the rest were dirt lanes.

One time, when I was coming home from a neighbor's house, a rattlesnake about 5 feet long was crossing from one side to another. I was running and shouting, "Oh, a rattlesnake!" One of my neighbors heard me hollering. He came out with his shotgun and killed that rattlesnake.

But you could go off and leave your house open and find it the same way.

The black families built the homes and paid rent on the land. My father collected the $3 a month rent for the owner. He also made $2 to $3 a day running the "Afromobiles" at the Palm Beach Hotel. My mother did domestic work in hotels in the winter and in residences the rest of the year. Wash, iron, cook; she made $1.25 a day.

We had school at the St. Paul A.M.E. Church in the Styx, and we had birthday parties and picnics at the ocean. A woman and her husband had a dance hall in the Styx for adults. A man nicknamed "Rabbit" played ragtime music on the piano.

I moved out of the Styx in my teens. They just told us, "We want our

*EARLY SCHOOL
The first school for black children opened in 1894 at the Tabernacle Baptist Church. The school shown here was built around 1896 at Tamarind Avenue and Datura Street. Inez Peppers Lovett's first teaching job was at a school in Delray.* ■

*A STELLAR DAUGHTER*
*Charlie Lovett Ellington was only 8 when a car accident left her mother a widow. But Inez managed to send Charlie to college in Atlanta, and Charlie followed in her mother's footsteps and became an educator. She went on to manage the school system's north area special education office and head the local chapter of the National Urban League, among other activities.* ■

land." Then after we all moved out, they cleaned it out.

Was I sad? I didn't know the difference. I wasn't anything but a child.

West of the Dixie Highway in West Palm Beach was blacks. East of the highway was whites.

In downtown West Palm Beach, you couldn't go in any stores. Blacks weren't allowed to try on shoes, and we had to try on dresses back in the sewing room. No Negro was allowed to sit down and eat. They had a long counter and the white side had chairs but blacks had to stand. We couldn't go into the white theaters. There were black theaters on Rosemary Avenue. One time I went to a white church and the blacks had to sit upstairs.

All I ever knew was segregation, so it was all right with me.

I finished my high school and college at Spelman College in Atlanta. I paid $11 a month. Room, board, classes, *everything!*

I got my first job in Delray at the black elementary and high school. At that time, they would stop school in December so the black kids could pick beans, then reopen in June. I had to take a train to Delray at the beginning of the week, would stay at a lady's house down there, then take the train back to West Palm Beach on Friday. It was wilderness along the way; nothing but bushes.

I then worked in Boca Raton. That was a one-teacher school. I was principal and everything. It was a tiny black community along Dixie Highway.

I worked as a maid two winters, then taught four years at Industrial School, then Pleasant City Elementary, then Roosevelt Elementary.

We had moved in the 1920s to property along 20th Street. I still live there.

In the Depression, my husband, Charlie Lee Lovett, walked and walked and walked trying to get a job. One day, he said, "Well, I walked until I walked the bottoms of my shoes off, and I still don't have a job. I don't know what we're going to do." I wondered how I was going to eat. My uncle had a general store on Division and Fifth, and my mother asked him to hire my husband. Men were getting $12 a week.

My husband was killed in an automobile accident in 1935, heading out to the Glades. It was a Sunday night. I was in my home. My cousin brought me the message. Charlie (only child Charlie Ellington, a retired educator) was a little girl in the fourth grade. From then on I had to see about her by myself. My father had died in 1925. My mother died in 1948.

I never remarried. I just survived. That's all.

I retired in 1969 from Roosevelt Elementary. I taught 48 years in public schools.

When I retired, they were just getting into integration. I never had the least idea that I would live to see what I have seen in my days. I never had dreams that black folks would have the opportunities they have.

## INEZ PEPPERS LOVETT IN 1994

*She poses near her home, with Lake Mangonia in the background. She has lived in the area since she was 2 months old.* ■

# What happened to the Styx?

The circus came to town, and the Styx burned.

Or did it?

The black shantytown known as the Styx sprang up on County Road, north of the Royal Poinciana Hotel, in the 1890s to house the more than 2,000 black workers at Palm Beach's hotels.

Over the years, a legend developed that Henry Flagler was eager to oust the blacks so he could develop the land. He had the Styx condemned on health grounds. Then, he hired a circus to come to West Palm Beach, gave black residents passes, and while they were there, burned their homes down.

Another legend places the incident on Guy Fawkes Day, Nov. 5, 1906. It says the blacks were at celebrations in West Palm Beach, and when they returned the next day, their homes were burned.

"I don't remember any fire," Inez Peppers Lovett, born in

1895, says. "Maybe they did burn the shacks, but if they did, it was after everyone had already moved away."

In February 1994, T.T. Reese Jr., of the pioneer Dimick/Reese family, wrote to *The Palm Beach Post* "to lay these questions to rest."

First, Flagler didn't own the property. The Bradley brothers, who owned the Beach Club casino, bought the 30 acres around 1910 and by February 1912 had cut the land into 230 residential lots for the Floral Park development.

In 1912, Reese says, Bradley ordered his father to move the residents out. He says his father gave them at least two weeks.

"I remember watching the squatters and their belongings going across the old wooden bridge with hand carts and other carriers," Reese says. After everyone had vacated the property, my dad brought in gardeners from the Beach Club and cleared the land, piled up the trash and burned it on the spot."

*THE STYX, AROUND 1900*
*On the left is the dance hall, where a man nicknamed "Rabbit" played ragtime on the piano.* ■

# West Palm Beach & Palm Beach in 1907

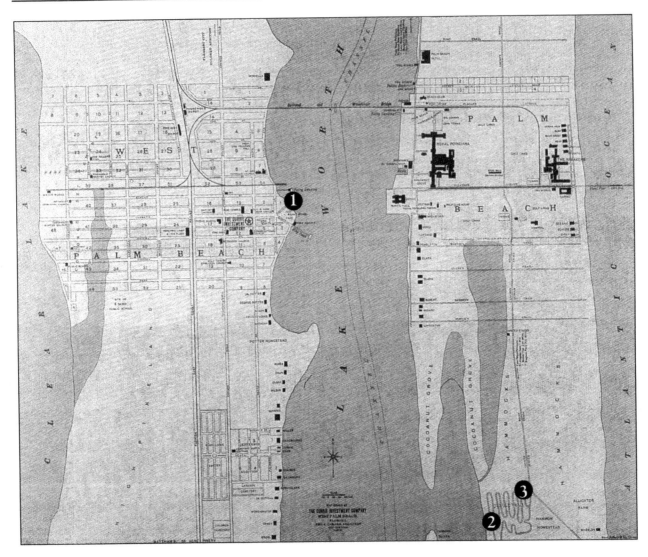

The Currie Investment Company produced this map of West Palm Beach and Palm Beach points of interest to attract real estate investors. Homes of prominent citizens are marked, such as the George Potter homestead and Franklin Sheen's home, Windella, in West Palm Beach. ■

## 1 City Park

At the foot of Clematis Street was City Park, the center of activity in early West Palm Beach. Concerts were held here (a band shell and rows of seats were built later), and the merchants along Narcissus and Clematis would even have impromptu ballgames in the park when business was slow. The first library — the "free reading room" — was in the two-story building at right. It was originally located in the Union Congregational Church at Datura and Olive, but in 1900, Palm Beach yachtsman C.J. Clarke donated the former Yacht Club building. Book lovers passed a hat and Henry Flagler gave $100, and the building was floated across from Palm Beach to City Park. In 1924, a new Spanish-style building opened at the east end of the park, but too many books and termites doomed that structure. The current library opened in 1962.

## 2 Alligator Joe

No trip to West Palm Beach was complete without a stop at Alligator Joe's bungalow off the Jungle Trail in Palm Beach (where the Everglades Club golf course is now). Alligator Joe is shown here with a pet sea cow in 1905.

## 3 Jungle Trail

Literally a jungle, the trail was a long and winding road just wide enough for a double "wheelchair" or "Afromobile." This was one of Palm Beach's biggest tourist attractions — particularly when a snake or alligator would cross the trail.

IN THE GARDEN OF HIS PALM BEACH HOME, 1994
*Like his grandfather, Tommy Reese grows dozens of types of plants in his back
yard, even coconut palms. In Cap Dimick's day, the young palms "were so close
together you couldn't see me if I was standing right next to you," Reese says.* ■

# Thomas Tipton Reese Jr.
## Grandson of Cap Dimick,
## Palm Beach's first hotelier and first mayor

Tommy Reese provided these memoirs in interviews in 1988 and May 1994.

This was just about the best place on earth to grow up — a Shangri-La for kids. There was fishing and hunting and all this open space. Just about everything was jungle and marsh or sand and palmetto.

When I was a youngster, my family lived with my grandparents at their home, Orangerie, which ran from the lake to the ocean just north of Wells Road in Palm Beach. My mother was Cap's daughter, Belle. Later, we moved to Sunset Avenue in Palm Beach.

Every morning, I'd wake up early, ride my bike down to where I had run trap lines for 'coons — down by where the Colony Hotel is now. I'd tend my traps and skin my raccoons — I got $12 a hide in the winter. Then I'd clean up, eat my breakfast and ride my bike over the wooden bridge to the Central School. I would have to push my cycle through sand from Dixie Highway to the hill up there, but I would be in school when the bell rang.

When I was about 7, I had a stand in front of E.R. Bradley's Beach Club. I called Mr. Bradley "Uncle Ed," since our families were close friends. I sold lucky beans, all kinds of flowers, mangoes, avocados and other fruit, and even baby alligators. I'd sell whatever I could find.

Uncle Ed's wife, Agnes, was a real fine lady. Every afternoon around 4:30, she'd call down from her house next to the Beach Club, "Come on up, kids," and we'd traipse in there barefooted and have ice cream and macaroons. She had one servant who did nothing but straighten the tassels on her Persian rugs.

All day, there were 15 to 20 wheelchairs in front of the Beach Club to take patrons back to their rooms at the hotels or to ride them down the winding "Jungle Trail" or up to Cragin's "Garden of Eden." The Jungle

TOMMY REESE, AGE 12
*He spent his youth biking, hunting, fishing, swimming — and making lots of mischief around Palm Beach.* ■

Trail was a two- to three-hour ride, at a charge of $2 an hour for the double chair and $1 for the single. The trail was just a foot up from the marsh, and alligators and moccasins would cross the road — quite an excitement for folks who aren't use to them.

At Alligator Joe's place about halfway along the trail, there were nearly 100 crocodiles and alligators, a panther and a bear. Everybody would go down to watch an old Seminole Indian wrestle with the alligators.

My grandfather had one of the first Ford Model T's here on the island. That was around 1912. On holidays, the whole family would get in the car and go see Uncle Harvey Geer out in the boondocks at the corner of Belvedere Road and Parker Avenue in West Palm Beach. We would start out in the Model T Ford about 6 in the morning and go across the bridge. U.S. 1 was all shell rock and about as wide as a desk and full of potholes. When you got to Belvedere, there was a sign that said, "Turn here for

E.R. BRADLEY'S FAMOUS BEACH CLUB
Col. Edward Riley Bradley was a friend of the Reese family. The Kentucky horseman opened the Beach Club in 1899 and broke American tradition when he admitted women to his gambling casino. Bradley closed the place in 1945; he died a year later. Joseph P. Kennedy lamented, "Palm Beach has lost its zipperoo." ▪

Harvey Geer." You would turn west on Belvedere and it was all sand. You got out, and you pushed and you shoved. By noon, we would get to Harvey's place, have a quick lunch and then get back in our car. We would push and shove until we got to Olive Avenue. Then we would get back home about 4 or 5 in the afternoon. That was an all-day ride.

I was a rascal when I was a kid. One Sunday, my friends and I went onto all the big estates and took the keys to the spigots that controlled the sprinklers. Well, on Monday, when the caretakers tried to water the lawns, they couldn't do it. They got ahold of Joe Borman, the chief of police, who said, "I know where those keys are. I'll be back in 30 minutes." Then he came over to my house and said, "Tommy, hand over the keys." He knew it was me.

I was born Dec. 13, 1907 — Friday the 13th — and I've been mischievous ever since.

Tommy Reese lives in Palm Beach, in a house he and his wife Helen built in 1949. Helen was the daughter of Franklin Sheen, West Palm Beach's city engineer and the man who surveyed Okeechobee Road in 1909. The couple grew up together — "she was the youngest baby at my first birthday party," he recalls — and shared a love of fishing and the outdoors. They married in 1927. Reese worked with his brother, Claude Dimick Reese, in the family's real estate and insurance business. Claude — like his grandfather and his father, Thomas Tipton Reese — became a mayor of Palm Beach. He died at age 87 in 1984, after serving 56 years in town government (18 as mayor and 38 as a council member). Helen Reese died in February 1993. Her husband still refers to her as "my Helen," and her photograph faces his favorite easy-chair. Their daughter, Jane Reese Hunter, lives in Sanford, Fla.

*Helen Reese*

*UNVEILING CAP'S STATUE, 1920*
*This statue of Cap Dimick, now on Royal Palm Way in Palm Beach, was originally in West Palm Beach. Dedicating it were Ella Geer Dimick, Cap's wife (seated with her great-grandson Claude Dimick Reese Jr. in her lap), Belle Dimick Reese (Tommy's mother, at left) and Claude Dimick Reese (Tommy's older brother and long-time mayor of Palm Beach).* ■

# The first newspapers

## My, how things change . . . and stay the same

A sampling of column items from *The Gazetteer*.

July 4, 1894. Black bear killed on fresh water lake.

July 11, 1894. Jas. K. Marvin opened a grocery store.

July 14, 1894. A hermit discovered on the shores of Lake Osborne.

Aug. 15, 1894. The city jail gets its first lodger — a Bohemian.

Sept. 10, 1894: Gazetteer threatened with a libel suit.

Sept. 15, 1894. Ed. Brinkerhoff and Jos. Lytzen, plumbers, found insensible in an iron water tank which they were painting, with asphaltum, from its fumes, by the water boy; the most careful treatment restored them.

Sept. 26, 1894. Hohn Brave, chief engineer on the Steamer Sweeney, catches a fish never seen before.

Oct. 27, 1894. First marriage in West Palm Beach, D. McCarley to Miss Elizabeth Boatright.

Dec. 12, 1894. New York papers reach us in 40 hours; six months ago it took from four to six weeks.

May 18, 1895. Threats to hickory-whip editor of *Gazetteer* by a county official.

June 22, 1895. First carload of keg beer arrives.

Aug. 24, 1895. Meetings called in the interest of law and order; after much talk nothing is done.

## The first editors: Colorful lives, violent deaths

C.M. Gardner, editor of the city's first newspaper, *The Gazetteer*, cast the first vote for incorporation. Things went downhill from there.

He had trouble getting the city to pay for its legal announcements, began an unpopular anti-alcohol crusade, was threatened with a libel suit and later with a hickory whip, charged with criminal libel but cleared by a grand jury, and burned out of business in the second of the two catastrophic 1896 fires.

*Guy Metcalf*

In a brawl, rival publisher Guy Metcalf of *The Tropical Sun* hit him in the head with a printer's mallet, sending him in a sickening sprawl down a flight of stairs.

Finally, Gardner was confronted in 1900 by a 17-year-old boy, who was fed up with Gardner's barbs and said, "Cross that line and you'll be shot."

Gardner did. And he was.

Metcalf, meanwhile, had an equally lively career. He pressed Dade County to build the first road to Miami, in 1892. After selling his paper to the Flagler empire, he helped establish a state railroad commission, earning the scorn of the Flagler forces. He helped overpower opposition to the school complex on "the hill," then became county school superintendent in 1917.

In February 1918, Metcalf was arrested for forging a bill for $333.49 for science equipment. The next morning he was found sitting in a chair in the vault at his office, dead of a bullet to the head. He was 52.

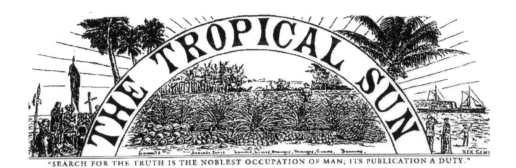

"SEARCH FOR THE TRUTH IS THE NOBLEST OCCUPATION OF MAN; ITS PUBLICATION A DUTY."

## West Palm Beach's newspapers

**The Tropical Sun:** Founded as *Indian River News* in Melbourne, Feb. 24, 1887; renamed *The Tropical Sun* and moved to Juno, March 18, 1891; moved to West Palm Beach, January 1895. Sold to Henry Flagler interests, 1902. Moved to Palm Beach, 1941. Bought in 1950 by Elias J. Chalhub, owner of Carefree Bowling Alley and theater, and moved back to West Palm Beach. Folded in 1956.

**The Gazetteer:** 1893-February 1896; destroyed in downtown fire. Equipment used to start *Daily Lake Worth News*, Feb. 12, 1897; became *Palm Beach Daily News* ("Shiny Sheet") in 1907.

**The Weekly Lake Worth News:** 1894 to 1908.

**Palm Beach Independent:** December 1925 to August 1929.

### The Weekly Lake Worth News.
West Palm Beach, Florida, December, Nineteen Hundred.

**The Palm Beach Post:** Founded as the weekly *Palm Beach County* in 1909; became the daily *The Palm Beach Post* in January 1916. Bought by casino magnate Col. E.R. Bradley, 1934; sold to Perry Publications, 1947. Sold to Cox Newspapers, July 1, 1969.

**The Palm Beach Times:** Founded Sept. 8, 1922. Bought by E.R. Bradley, 1934; sold to Perry Publications, 1947; sold to Cox Newspapers, July 1, 1969. *Times* renamed *The Evening Times* in 1979. *The Times* merged with *The Palm Beach Post* in 1987.

WORLD NEWS
BY THE
ASSOCIATED PRESS

# THE PALM BEACH POST

LARGEST DAILY
CIRCULATION IN
PALM BEACH COUNTY

VOL. XXI: No. 324     WEST PALM BEACH, FLORIDA, WEDNESDAY, JANUARY 1, 1930     DAILY, FIVE CENTS. SUNDAY, TEN CENTS.

# The law . . .

POLICEMAN'S
BEST FRIEND
*Deputy Sheriff S.A.*
*Barfield with his sidekick,*
*Jeff, around 1915.*
*Barfield was one of the*
*deputies who sought*
*gangster John Ashley (see*
*Page 93).* ■

SHOWING OFF
THE NEW FIRE
EQUIPMENT, 1911
*The first central fire sta-*
*tion and the first horse-*
*drawn ladder truck*
*debuted to much fanfare*
*in 1905. By 1911, West*
*Palm Beach's fire depart-*
*ment had its first motor-*
*ized firetruck — and, to*
*drive it, the first two full-*
*time, paid firefighters.* ■

## A tough town for police and firemen

Law and order in pioneer West Palm Beach was kept by a town marshal, who also had to collect taxes. A police department wasn't formed until 1919.

The first marshal, W.L. Torbert, who had to contend with rowdy Banyan Street, was paid an impressive $60 a month. Torbert was suspended in October 1895 after killing a black man while trying to arrest him. His successor got only $50, with a 25-cent bonus for each impounded dog.

Within two weeks of the city's incorporation, the "Flagler Alerts" volunteer fire department was organized. It would be 1902, after another calamitous downtown fire, before an official department was created.

When The Breakers burned June 10, 1903, the firefighters raced across the railroad bridge with a hand-drawn hose cart and 500 feet of hose. The tender demanded 5 cents from each man. The firefighters, trying to decide between exasperation and amazement, stood on the bridge fishing their pockets for nickels while The Breakers burned. The town later wrote to the Flagler interests, asking the toll be waived for firemen.

The first firehouse was built at Datura and Poinsettia, now Dixie Highway. It opened with fanfare and a parade on the Fourth of July, 1905.

# . . . & the lawless

## Banyan Street in the 1890s:
## Booze, brothels and brawls

If you wanted whiskey, women or trouble in early West Palm Beach, there was just one place to go: Banyan Street, the East Coast's answer to the Wild West.

The only street in town where alcohol was allowed, Banyan was so notorious it was nicknamed "Whiskey Street." Saloons operated around the clock — right next to gambling halls and brothels.

They all catered to the rough-hewn workers who built Palm Beach's hotels, but even town leaders got stung by Banyan's temptations.

West Palm Beach's first mayor, John Earman, almost got kicked out of office in 1895 when he was charged with "being with a certain prostitute called 'Specks' and being in a state of intoxication." Earman denied the charges, and they were dismissed a month later.

But that was nothing compared to the case of Sam Lewis.

Lewis tended bar at the corner of Olive and Banyan. Word was he came from Texas, where he'd killed some men. After a while, his boss bought a saloon in Lemon City, now in North Miami, and sent Lewis to run it.

There, in July 1895, he confronted John Highsmith, former tax collector for Dade County, possibly over a poker game. Highsmith told Lewis if he felt it was honorable to shoot an unarmed man, he could go ahead. Lewis did. George Davis, Highsmith's nephew, turned and ran, and Lewis shot him in the back.

Lewis fled to the Bahamas, then hijacked a boat back to Florida to hide out with friends. A posse went looking for him. Ret McGregor shattered Lewis' leg with gunfire; Lewis killed McGregor. He was sent to the county jail in Juno.

Afraid that Lewis' Banyan Street pals would spring him, a dozen vigilantes headed to Juno, shot a jailer dead, pulled Lewis out, hanged him from a telegraph pole and riddled him with bullets.

In 1904, fed up with Banyan's squalor, local women called in "the Kansas Cyclone" — Carry Nation, the 6-foot, black-clad, Bible-clutching matron of temperance who smashed bars across America with her holy hatchet.

The city finally changed Banyan to First Street in 1925.

Then the locals started calling it "Thirst Street."

*CARRY NATION HITS BANYAN*
*She was big and she was mean — but the temperance crusader's visit to wild Banyan Street in 1904 didn't change anything.* ■

UNION CONGREGATIONAL CHURCH
Founded in 1894, one of the church's missions was to help tame the wild Banyan Street crowd. ▪

# "A church in the heart of the city"

ST. ANN CATHOLIC CHURCH
Built in 1895 at Rosemary Avenue and Datura Street, it was moved a few years later to its current location at Olive Avenue and Second Street. ▪

Now, you need a church.

Missionaries worked the Lake Region as early as 1883 and Palm Beach's Bethesda-by-the-Sea was founded in 1889. Blacks founded Tabernacle Missionary Baptist and Payne Chapel A.M.E. in the Styx in Palm Beach in 1893.

In 1894, Bethesda members organized Union Congregational Church for West Palm Beach and arranged to buy a site at the northwest corner of Olive and Datura streets. When Henry Flagler heard this, he donated the property, saying, "There will always be a church in the heart of the city."

On a Saturday afternoon, as ferries from Palm Beach unloaded workers at the foot of raucous Banyan Street, church organizers held out a basket and collected portions of pay envelopes. At least one saloon-keeper's wife, unhappy about the loss of commerce, let them have it in language that was anything but God-like.

The money bought lumber, which was stolen the first night — by the saloonkeepers, some said — prompting volunteers to stand watch.

Union Congregational was followed by St. Ann (Catholic), Holy Trinity (Episcopal), First Baptist and United Methodist. The town council paid $24 for the Methodist church's bell, which doubled as a fire alarm.

Jewish residents founded a community center in 1918, and the first synagogue came in 1926.

## ❋
# *Pioneer Profile*

# Haley Mickens & Alice Frederick Mickens

*by Alice E. Moore, their foster daughter*

Dr. Moore, a retired Palm Beach County teacher, wrote this "pioneer history of my family" in 1989. She met West Palm Beach pioneer Haley Mickens and his second wife, Alice Frederick Mickens, when she was a child and became their foster daughter.

In the Bible, we find these words, "Your old men shall dream dreams, your young men shall see visions."

This young man, Haley Mickens, had visions. Born in Monticello, Fla., he visualized coming to South Florida to begin a new life. His quest led him to the "Styx," now called Palm Beach.

His grandmother said to him before he left home, "Son, wherever you go, stick to the church." But in the Styx, can you imagine? There was no church, no school, no cars, but plenty of mosquitoes, palm trees, pineapples, virgin soil and beautiful weather. I often heard my father say that God was in the plan.

So it was in 1893, while my father and some of his comrades sat by an open fire in the Styx, he said, "Fellows, we could at least have a prayer meeting." So they did, and out of this meeting, Payne Chapel A.M.E. Church was started.

You see, God used my Dad to bring about Payne Chapel.

Then Henry M. Flagler wanted to make Palm Beach the playground of America.

Flagler conceived the idea of establishing a commercial city on the west side of Lake Worth and all of the black people living in the Styx were pushed out. My dad had to seek a new home.

The black people came over and built shacks or stayed in shacks provided for them until they could do better. Finally, Dad built a house where he and his first wife, Lula, lived until her death.

*PAYNE CHAPEL*
*In 1893, Haley Mickens founded a church, called Bethel, in the Styx. In 1894, the name became Payne Chapel A.M.E., and in 1895, plans were made to build this church at the corner of Tamarind Avenue and Banyan Street. In the mid-'20s, the current, Gothic revival style church was built on Ninth Street.* ■

HALEY
MICKENS

*Mickens was an
ardent church work-
er and a member of
the Masonic Lodge.
"To him, a true
Mason was a good
citizen," Alice
Moore remembers.
Mickens died in
1950 at age 77.* ■

Wheelchairs were very familiar vehicles on the streets of Palm Beach. Not the wheelchair as we think of it today, but a chair mounted on three wheels and usually propelled by blacks to transport millionaires over the island.

Now, Mr. E.R. Bradley, a Kentucky colonel, owned what was called the Beach Club. I don't know how he came to know Dad. I do know that he became interested enough in Dad to give him the wheelchair concession, thus allowing him to make a living. Dad, in turn, felt very grateful, thus he felt it his duty to transport the colonel and members of his family when needed.

Mr. Bradley must have possessed a great deal of humor.

One day a member of the club told Mr. Bradley that his restaurant prices were at least 10 percent higher than any other eating place in the world, whereupon the colonel replied, "That may be true, but our meals are 90 percent better."

Now let me tell you about Alice Gertrude Frederick Mickens, the most beautiful person I have ever known. She became my father's wife on Nov. 19, 1917.

After emancipation, her parents lived on a big farm in South Carolina, where they grew cotton. I'm told that when voting became a privilege, her father was asked by a white man to vote for his candidate, but her father refused.

Thereupon this man sharply replied, "If you don't vote for John Doe, then you will not use my gin for your cotton."

Well, no gin, no cotton harvested, no money.

It was then that her father had to seek a new life.

He settled in Bartow, Fla., having been called by God to minister to people. Her mother, Frances, thought her childbearing age was over. Here she was in Florida, away from her doctor (she said childbearing was difficult for her), but guess what? She had a baby girl, and they named her Alice Gertrude Frederick.

Shortly after Alice, who I call Sister, was born, her father became ill and died. He said to Frances, "I will not be here to care for you and baby Alice, but the boys will take care of you." And, sure enough, they did.

Soon, Sister's brother Nathaniel, "Nat" as he was affectionately called, moved to West Palm Beach and sent for his mother. And so the West Palm Beach story begins.

Sister's mother, Frances, was so angelic. She went to church, visited the sick and shut-in and nurtured her family.

Sister, by this time, was in and out of the city attending school at Spelman College in Atlanta. When she returned to West Palm Beach, she found that her mother's health was not good, and her brother asked if she would stay here and nurture mother.

## ALICE FREDERICK MICKENS AT HOME

*Mrs. Mickens poses in the entryway of the home her husband built for her in 1917 at Fourth Street and Division Avenue. The home has changed little in the past 77 years and is now on the National Register of Historic Places.* ■

ALICE MOORE
AS A YOUNG
WOMAN

Moore lived across the
street from Haley and
Alice Mickens, and she
would often see Mr.
Mickens working in the
yard as she walked to
school. She soon joined
their family, caring for
Alice Mickens' mother
and, later, Mrs.
Mickens. "Fate led this
little girl to us," her
foster parents always
said. ■

Sister became active in her church, playing for worship services and Sunday school, and teaching adult Bible class. She also taught music in the home.

This was a very small town, everybody knew everybody. Since both were of the same faith, in the same church, she met Mr. Mickens, and they married. He built their home at 801 4th St. in 1917.

Sister, like her mother, was always helping others. They both believed they must share. And by this time, the National Association of Colored Women's Clubs was trying to organize throughout the United States. Sister was asked to serve as state organizer. This is how she met Mary McLeod Bethune, founder and president of Bethune Cookman College, who started her school with five little girls and faith in God.

They met early one morning when Sister boarded a Jim Crow car at the F.E.C. Railroad in West Palm Beach. She was going to Miami on a mission of club work, and Dr. Bethune was on a mission for her college. As she boarded the train, Dr. Bethune roused from her very uncomfortable position and said, "Aren't you Alice Mickens?"

Dr. Bethune knew of the good work Sister had done and invited her to visit the college. This Sister did, and the rest is history.

They were friends forever. Our home was her home; her home was our home.

Alice Frederick Mickens served as trustee and Dr. Bethune's backbone at Bethune Cookman College for more than 30 years.

She received an honorary doctorate from the college in 1971, and a lecture hall was named after her in 1983.

She dined with Eleanor Roosevelt, opened her home to Nobel Peace prize recipient and former U.N. Undersecretary Ralph Bunche, and helped persuade the state to build a home for wayward black adolescent girls so they would not be placed with women criminals. A cottage on the grounds in Lowell still bears her name.

When Dr. Mickens died on Jan. 19, 1988, three months short of her 100th birthday, hundreds mourned her for two hours at Payne Chapel.

That day, Alice Moore wrote, "Reassuring herself that the master would say, 'Well done, thy good and faithful servant,' she grasped the outstretched hands of her long departed husband, Mr. Haley Mickens, and they faded into the gleaming light of the Great Beyond."

ALICE MOORE, WITH A PORTRAIT OF HER BELOVED "SISTER"

*"Before Dad died, he said to Sister, 'I am going to leave you, but I know Alice will take care of you,' " Moore recalls. She did just that, becoming a faithful companion, an elementary school teacher and — following in Sister's footsteps — a civic leader.* ■

# The first merchants

By 1900, you could buy all the modern conveniences in West Palm Beach.

Carl Schrebnick's Honest Profit House — "the largest store in town" — bragged about its "dry goods and gents' furnishings." M.E. Gruber, the "hardware and furniture man," claimed he had "anything required to furnish a house." And Johnny Jumper, a Seminole Indian, was selling buckskin moccasins and rattlesnake belts at L.A. Willson's on Clematis.

Those stores are all gone now. But some of the old-timers remain.

Who could grow up in West Palm Beach and not buy Bass Weejuns at J.C. Harris? Or a hammer at Sewell's Hardware ("try Sewell, he might have it")? Or linens at Pioneer?

Anthony's has been selling the latest in fashion for nearly 100 years. Way back in the early years, their slogan was "Anthony's shoes are silent salesmen."

So much has changed on Clematis Street since 1900, but the faces and places on the next pages are still as comforting and comfortable as those shoes.

ON CLEMATIS, 1899

*M.E. Gruber's Hardware Store was a big attraction in the early years (Gruber is second from right in the bow tie). This spot became the site of the Palm Beach Mercantile ("The Big Store"), now the Harris Music building. To the east of Gruber's was the Dimick & Riegel drugstore, later the site of the Citizens building.* ■

# FURNITURE.

The Largest and Best Selected stock south of Jacksonville.

Bedroom and Parlor Sets,

Chairs,
Bed Springs,
Baby Carriages,
Go-Carts.

Anything Required to Furnish a House.

## M. E. GRUBER
### The Hardware and Furniture Man

**For the Kitchen.**
There is nothing lacking.
STOVES
of the highest grade and most modern styles.
Kitchen Furnishings of all kinds.
CROCKERY
to suit your every taste.

**HARDWARE**
of every description for everybody.
TOOLS.
of all descriptions.
PAINTS
of the best kinds.
Sash, Doors, Blinds.
If you are going to build a house, or paint a house, or furnish a house, you can get what you want at GRUBER'S.

AMMUNITION
—and—
FISHING TACKLE

The Best Goods and the Best Stock in the country. Everything you need for a hunting or fishing trip.

If there is ANYTHING you want, go to

## GRUBER'S.
West Palm Beach, Fla.

---

*We Are Selling*

# GRASS HATS

*By The Hundreds*

You Had Better Get in Line

## PRICE $1.00

## ANTHONY BROTHERS.
### Jefferson Block, West Palm Beach.

Palm Beach,          Miami, Fla

---

While in Palm Beach Don't Fail to Visit the

## ·Florida· Alligator· Farm·
### and Alligator Joe.

**Hundreds of Crocodiles and Alligators Always in Sight.**

Our pools are alive with them; they literally swarm over everything. A sight you see but once in a lifetime. Instructive as well as amusing. Special features two afternoons in the week. Don't miss seeing Alligator Joe capture a 'gator single handed. We have on sale (made from skins raised and tanned on the farm)

**All Kinds of Alligator Goods and Novelties,**

Seminole and Florida Curios, in our immense Curio Hall. A house covered entirely with the largest of Tarpon Scales. Call and see us; you will be pleased.

ALLIGATOR JOE & CO., Proprietors.

J. J. BOWEN, Manager.

---

Crayons.                    Water Colors.

### ⇐Richard E. Resler,⇒

## Portrait and Landscape Photographer

Clematis Avenue, Opposite the Bank,

·West · Palm · Beach, · Florida.·

*Developing and Printing for Amateurs.*

---

## A. L. HAUGH,
—DEALER IN—

# BICYCLES
AND
BICYCLE SUNDRIES.

GENERAL BICYCLE REPAIRING.

☞FIRST-CLASS WORK AND STOCK.☜

CLEMATIS AVENUE, OPPOSITE THE BANK,
WEST PALM BEACH.

---

B. M. POTTER,
—DEALER IN—

# BICYCLES

Bicycle Sundries, Ammunition and Sporting Goods.

PALM BEACH.    West Palm Beach, Florida.

Special attention given to Bicycle, Gun, Lock, and General Mechanical Repairs.

---

## L. A. WILSON.

### FOR BUCKSKIN MOCCASINS
GENUINE SEMINOLE INDIAN SUITS,
AND RATTLE-SNAKE BELTS,

CALL ON
JOHNNY JUMPER, the Seminole Indian,
at L. A. Wilson's Shoe Shop, where you can get any kind of Footwear made to order, and all leather Repairing neatly and promptly done. Also a Full Line of imported Mexican Hats.
Corner of Clematis Avenue and Olive Streets, near the Bank.

Ads from The Weekly Lake Worth News, 1900. ▪

# White shoes:
# Born and worn in Palm Beach

**E.D. ANTHONY & FAMILY, 1924**

*Emile D. Anthony ran the Anthony's empire in West Palm Beach from 1914 through World War II. In the boom years — 1914 to 1925 — he operated 12 stores. This photograph of Anthony, his wife, Gertrude, and their children was taken at their home at 315 Dyer Road. Note that Anthony is wearing the "Poinciana uniform" — navy blazer and white pants. The children are, from left: Carl, Emile Jr., M. Pope ("Ham") and Cornelia. Emile Sr. eventually turned the stores over to his children (he died in 1965), and for years, Emile Jr. ran the men's department, Ham ran the ladies' department and Carl handled the business end (and, later, Anthony's Groves). Cornelia Anthony Sned died in 1984, but her brothers are all still living in the area.* ■

The height of high-society fashion for men 100 years ago was the "Poinciana Uniform" — a navy sport coat, white pants, white shoes and a straw boater.

It's still in style, and it all started with the Anthony brothers, who opened their first store in West Palm Beach in 1895 and also had a store in Henry Flagler's Royal Poinciana Hotel.

Before the Anthonys, there were no white shoes — shoes were either brown, black or gray.

But black shoes didn't seem right with the men's light trousers and the sheer, white cotton dresses that ladies wore to afternoon tea in the Poinciana's Coconut Grove. So, A.P. Anthony (older brother of Emile Anthony, who ran the Anthony's stores for years) asked his shoe manufacturer to start making white shoes — for the ladies and the gents.

After much persuading, the manufacturer agreed.

Soon, white shoes became popular all around the country, sparking the famous fashion rule: You can wear white shoes only after Easter and before Labor Day.

Everywhere that is, except Palm Beach, where white can still be right in February, just as it was in Flagler's time.

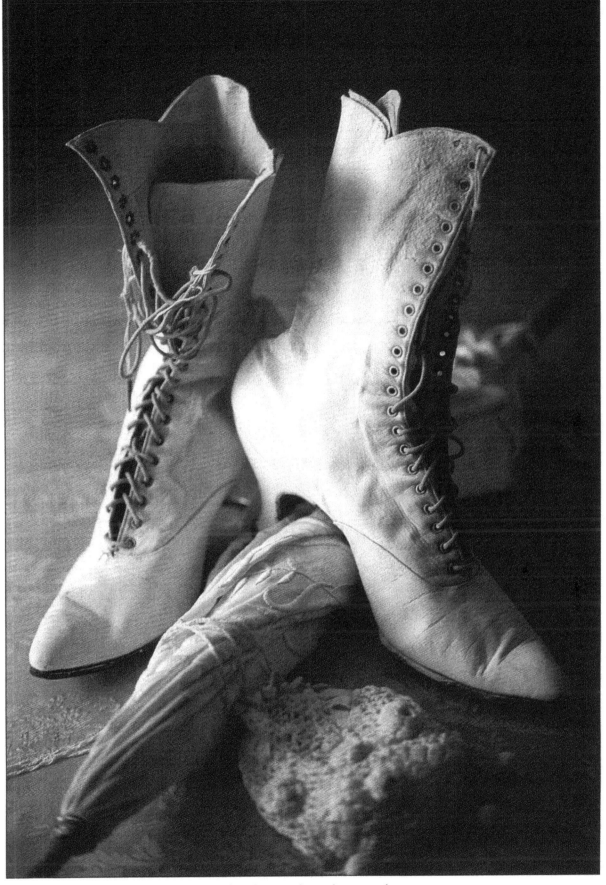

*White shoes from 1895, with a parasol and purse from that period.* ■

J.C. HARRIS, 1903

When you want Bass Weejuns, you go to J.C. Harris. Everybody who grew up in West Palm Beach knows that. And when you get there, you know who will wait on you: one of J.C. Harris' boys. Today, four Harrises work in the family store, which has been on Clematis since 1913 (the first 10 years were spent on Datura Street): Robert C. Harris, 70 (right), son of founder James C. Harris, and his two sons, James (second from right) and John (far left). Robert K. Harris, son of the late Charles R. Harris (Robert's brother), is second from left. J.C. Harris created a custom tassel loafer (shoe at left) for Bass in the mid-'40s, and Bass has a version of the shoe in its line today (shoe at right). In the middle: A photo of founder J.C. Harris. ■

## PIONEER, 1912

George Greenberg, 79, runs the store his father, Max, founded. Pioneer Linens is patronized by people around the globe (and plenty of Palm Beach celebrities). "You see those customers over there?" Greenberg whispers. "They came here all the way from Sao Paulo, Brazil." ◼

## ANTHONY'S, 1895

The Anthony brothers became prominent in West Palm Beach. Augustus P. Anthony ran the Anthony's stores in the early years, then his younger brother, Emile, took over. At top right, the flagship store in the early 1920s. At right, Anthony's current president, Pope Anthony, son of M. Pope ("Ham") Anthony and grandson of Emile. ◼

SHEEN FAMILY, ON THE LAKEFRONT, AROUND 1910

Franklin Sheen, an engineer for Henry Flagler's Florida East Coast Model Land Company, came to West Palm Beach in 1893 and became a prominent citizen. He was county surveyor for 10 years, and he named the town of Pompano Beach because he caught so many pompano there. His home on the lakefront, Windella, was on the site where Rosarian Academy is today. Here, the Sheen family poses on their lawn around 1910: from left, wife Jessie Griffin Sheen, Franklin Sheen, the Sheens' daughter Helen, an unidentified relative, son Marion, an unidentified boy, and sons Franklin Jr. and Julian. By the time this photo was taken, Sheen was in ill health — he became sick while building Okeechobee Road the year before, according to his son-in-law, T.T. Reese Jr. He died of tuberculosis in 1917. ■

THE GATES CHILDREN, ON OKEECHOBEE ROAD, AROUND 1912

*Charles Frederick Gates and his wife, Alma, moved to West Palm Beach from Montana in 1910 when their youngest daughter, Sarah, was 1. A couple years later, they lined up the children for this snapshot: Sarah first, followed by Allegra, Russell, Lula, Frederick, Louise and Harlan. They lived on L Street, near where this photo was taken. Okeechobee Road was built out to Military Trail in 1909, and Sarah Gates Carroll, now 85, remembers that Clear Lake ran right up to the road. The tower of the Central School is in the background. Three of the siblings are still alive: Sarah, who still lives in West Palm Beach, Allegra and Lula.* ■

# The gates to eternity

When Henry Flagler built Woodlawn Cemetery, it became a tourist attraction. A St. Augustine *Tatler* item from January 1905 described how socialites would spend afternoons touring the Woodlawn grounds, with its rock roads and "rows of oleanders, Australian pines and crotons."

It wasn't the city's first graveyard; several pioneers had been buried across the street under what is now the Norton Gallery of Art. Some graves remain there, though others were moved to Woodlawn.

Flagler bought the Woodlawn site, then a pineapple grove, and deeded it to the city with the understanding that he would one day be buried there. But a "selfish, narrow-minded, contentious crowd" in West Palm Beach "antagonized Mr. Flagler and finally drove him away to be buried," wrote James Rembert Anthony, eldest of the Anthony retailers, in 1936.

The final straw came when West Palm Beach residents tried to annex Palm Beach in 1911, forcing Palm Beach to incorporate. Flagler decided then and there he would rather rest in peace in St. Augustine.

His tomb is there inside Memorial Presbyterian Church, which he built in 1889 in memory of his daughter, Jennie Louise Benedict. Jennie had died from complications from childbirth. Buried next to him are his first wife, Mary Harkness Flagler, who died of tuberculosis in 1881, his daughter Jennie and Jennie's baby, Margery. Historian Jim Ponce of West Palm Beach, who is from St. Augustine, recalls that an emotional Flagler himself asked undertaker Raymond A. Ponce, Jim's father, to bury Margery in her mother's arms.

*Under the auditorium of the Norton Gallery of Art are at least two graves and perhaps dozens more. Descendants of these late pioneers still have access to their final resting places, though the public does not.* ■

## WOODLAWN CEMETERY

*"The main entrance to the beautiful Woodlawn Cemetery is guarded by a massive gate of iron, black with letters of bronze. The avenues are of that pure white splendor which is characteristic of all the roads in this vicinity," reads the back of this postcard from around 1906. The inscription on the gate says, "That which is so universal as death must be a blessing." Woodlawn Cemetery remains on Dixie Highway, between Belvedere and Okeechobee roads, but the iron gate is gone, replaced with concrete pillars in 1925.* ■

# What I remember . . .

"**I** have been around long enough to remember when Judge Burkhardt used to compose poetry and print it on his business envelopes, to advertise the old burg to some of the sick Yankees back up in Pennsylvania . . .

"I remember the old town when Sheen & Moses were the only real estate agents; when 'Doc' Liddy had his tooth-pulling establishment on Clematis Street, about where Hatch's perfume counter is now; when Carl Schrebnick and Max Sirkin were the only Jewish merchants in town, and C.W. Schmidt operated the only restaurant in the village . . .

"I remember when George Potter brought in the first auto, and when Curtis Barco sold and rented bicycles. I remember when the first 'flapper' hit town — a little blond stenographer who scandalized the whole town when she landed one of the prominent businessmen under the table, barking like a dog, at a party one night. Gee, but Dorothy was some gal."
— *From "Ruminations of an Old-Timer" by Charles R. Barfield, 1930*

"**D**o you remember when the business center was from Zapf's Place, then the Seminole Hotel, where they sold the big cold ones with foam on for 5 cents . . . "
— *From a letter to* The Palm Beach Post *by Mrs. R. D. Taylor, 1923.*
*(George Zapf was a colorful liquor dealer who had a block of businesses at Narcissus and Banyan.)*

"**I** remember when I'd have to call my mother to get permission to go fishing. I'd ring the town's central phone operator and say, 'Goldie, where's Mama?'

" 'Is this Frankie?,' Goldie would say. Then she'd find my mother and call me back in a few minutes to say, 'Frankie, your mother said not to go fishing today . . .' "
— *From a 1976* Palm Beach Times *interview with Franklin Sheen Jr.*

FROM FLORIDA, A BOOK PUBLISHED AROUND 1900
*This promotional photograph, touting the climate and beauty of West Palm Beach, was from a book created for Henry Flagler's Florida businesses.*

Where the water lilies bloom in March. Wm. Glenn's place, West Palm Beach, Florida.

SHEEN'S REAL ESTATE AGENCY
WEST PALM BEACH, FLORIDA
Handles the Best Bargains in Real Estate
Improved and Unimproved Properties, Lake and
Ocean Front Properties, Business Blocks, Residence
Lots, Orange Groves, Fruit and Vegetable Lands.

## RACING FOR REAL ESTATE

After Franklin Sheen got out of the surveying business (see Page 72), he got into the most popular field in town: real estate. His office was in the distinctive, cone-roofed building that originally housed the first bank in Dade County. The building was moved from Palm Beach to West Palm Beach in 1897. Sheen used this promotional postcard around 1915 — before con artists really did start selling swampland. ■

## Chapter 4

# The Boom

## 1913-1926

*Here is a city of the sun. Here is a city of summer breeze, an environment of Eden. And here is health and happiness and prosperity for those who listen to its call. And this city's people, content in the pure joy of living, bid you come and make your home among them.*

— Introduction to a special edition
of *The Palm Beach Post*, October 1922

It didn't take long for West Palm Beach to explode into prominence and prosperity. Everyone wanted a piece of the sun.

It was a nation freed from war, suddenly mobile, drawn by blue skies and warm waters and cheap land and mesmerized by the chance to slip in now and score big later.

Neighborhoods sprang up, and so did a few skyscrapers. Clematis Street thrived, with real-estate offices on both sides. Property values artificially doubled and tripled in the frenzy of demand.

Opportunists called "Binder Boys" poured in from up north. Packing into hotel rooms, they worked the sidewalks, making fortunes by buying and selling property they never saw while only having to put down the "binder" — the 10 percent deposit. The same tract of land might be sold over and over, increasing in value each time, as documents moved down the street toward the courthouse for posting.

From 1920 to 1927, the city's population quadrupled. And everything grew: the schools, the farming and sugar businesses in the Glades, the hotels and theaters. One January 1925 newspaper, 150 pages fat, contained 12 full-page advertisements in a row for developments.

In just five years, from 1920 to 1925, the city's total property value increased almost fivefold, from $13.6 million to $61 million. By 1929, it was at a boom-era high of $89 million.

*HEADING FOR A BUST?*
*Cartoon from a 1925* Palm
Beach Post. ■

# Key events, 1913 - 1926

**June 14, 1913:** Lake Worth incorporated.

**1914:** "Emergency Hospital," forerunner to Good Samaritan, founded.

**Dec. 14, 1914:** Woodlawn Cemetery deeded to city.

**1915:** New jail built on First Street, between Dixie Highway and railroad tracks. Women's Club building built on waterfront; still standing in 1994.

**April 30, 1915:** Broward County formed.

**July 1, 1915:** State legislature creates Lake Worth Inlet District, later Port of Palm Beach.

**April 15, 1916:** Pine Ridge Hospital for blacks opens at Fifth and Division streets.

**June 1916:** Evergreen Cemetery for blacks opens; cemeteries will stay segregated for a half-century.

**1917:** Industrial High School for blacks opens.

**April 1917:** New county courthouse opens.

**Aug. 7, 1917:** Okeechobee County formed.

**1919:** City creates police department, city manager position. First manager, Joseph Firth, hired Nov. 4, 1919. New city hall opens at Second Street and Dixie Highway.

**1920:** Population: Florida 968,470; Palm Beach County 18,654; West Palm Beach 8,659. City property value: $13.6 million.

**Jan. 18, 1920:** Port of Palm Beach opens.

*Good Samaritan Hospital.*

**May 19, 1920:** Good Samaritan, area's first permanent hospital, opens with 35 beds at 12th Street and the lakefront.

**July 21, 1920:** Town of Boynton incorporated; named Boynton Beach in July 1941.

**July 20, 1921:** Lantana incorporated.

**March 1922:** Pahokee incorporated.

**Sept. 29, 1922:** Riviera incorporated; renamed Riviera Beach in 1941.

**1923:** Palm Beach County fair moves to 56-acre site in Howard Park area.

**Nov. 16, 1923:** Kelsey City incorporated; renamed Lake Park June 15, 1939.

**1924-1925:** Height of real estate boom in South Florida.

*Florida counties in 1925*

**Jan. 26, 1924:** First permanent library building opens with 7,000 volumes; named Memorial Library to honor World War I dead.

**July 24, 1924:** Connors Highway opens. The road, running west along West Palm Beach Canal from 20 Mile Bend to Lake Okeechobee, then north around the lake, connects West Palm Beach and Glades community and creates the first cross-peninsula route. Connors Highway is now State Road 80 to Belle Glade and U.S. 98/441 around east shore of lake.

**Oct. 14, 1924:** High school football game between Palm Beach and Gainesville is first event ever at Municipal Athletic Field, later Wright Field and eventually Connie Mack Field.

**1925:** City property value: $61.7 million — 5-fold increase over 1920.

**1925:** City's two tallest buildings constructed: the 10-story Comeau, on Clematis Street, and the 14-floor Harvey building, on Datura Street.

**1925-1926:** West Palm Beach Canal opens from Lake Okeechobee.

**Jan. 25, 1925:** Seaboard Air Line Railway opens to West Palm Beach.

**Feb. 9, 1925:** Jupiter incorporated.

**March 18, 1925:** The Breakers burns again. The cause: a new-fangled curling iron.

**May 12, 1925:** Gulf Stream incorporated.

**May 26, 1925:** Boca Raton incorporated.

**May 30, 1925:** Martin County and Indian River County formed.

**October 1925:** A 23-square-mile area just west of the Seaboard Air Line railroad tracks — now the CSX tracks, adjacent to Interstate 95 — votes to become part of West Palm Beach. It votes to leave only four years later.

**December 1925:** First regular steamship service established at Port of Palm Beach.

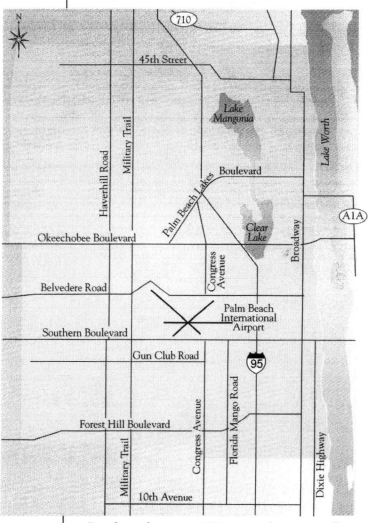

*City boundaries in 1926 — as shown in yellow on a 1994 base map. The 23-square-mile area west of what is now I-95 left the city in 1929.*

WEST PALM BEACH, 1922

*Palm Beach Mercantile (now the Harris Music building, built in 1916) is the tall building in the center of the photograph, on Clematis Street, across from The Palms Hotel. City Park is east of Clematis. The Women's Club (which was built in 1915 and still stands) is the square building on the Intracoastal at the tip of the curve, and the free reading room is just south of the Women's Club. Hotel Salt Air is the large building, bottom center.* ■

*Construction of the Palm Beach Mercantile building on Clematis, 1916.* ■

*Construction of the Comeau building on Clematis, 1925.* ∎

FLAGLER DRIVE, 1926
*The view from the "new Pennsylvania Hotel." In Palm Beach, the Alba Hotel (now The Biltmore) is the large building to the north and the Whitehall Hotel is the large building to the south (a hotel addition had been built onto Henry Flagler's mansion). The Royal Poinciana Hotel is in the middle.* ∎

# The boom hotels

Palm Beach was winter home for the cream of society.
Hotels for everyone else soon sprang up on the West Palm Beach waterfront.
Here are some of the more notable, most now gone.

The **Pennsylvania** (above) was built in 1925 on the site of
**The Holland** (below) at Evernia and the lakefront. The Holland
was built in 1899. For a brief time, the Pennsylvania was called the
Royal Worth, then the name was changed back to the Pennsyl-
vania. In 1964, the Pennsylvania became a residence hotel run by
Carmelite nuns. It was scheduled for demolition in 1994.

El Verano ("always summer"), January 1923 (right). Intracoastal Waterway north of library. Later the George Washington; now the Helen Wilkes Residence Hotel.

The Palms ("a temperance hotel"), Clematis and Narcissus, 1896. Razed 1926.

Keystone, Datura Street west of Dixie Highway, 1906. Demolished for a parking lot, 1968.

New Jefferson, Clematis and Olive, 1898; leveled in 1940s for office buildings.

Monterey ("on the hilltop"), Clematis and Sapodilla, February 1926. Demolished July 1976 for state office building.

Royal Palm ("for both transient and permanent guests"), Nov. 23, 1922, on Lakeview Avenue and Royal Park Bridge. Now Phillips Point.

Hibiscus Apartments, 1926, Hibiscus and Sapodilla. Placed on National Register of Historic Places, May 10, 1984. Demolished 1989.

Lakeview Manor, 208 Lakeview. Later a home for the elderly. Bulldozed June 1986.

Salt Air, Narcissus and Datura, Dec. 15, 1913. Later the site of the downtown Holiday Inn, which was demolished by implosion Jan. 1, 1994.

Dixie Court, 301 N. Dixie, April 1926. Demolished 1990. Now site of Palm Beach County Governmental Center.

# Carl Kettler:
# West Palm's movie man

CARL KETTLER
AND FAMILY
*Kettler's wife, Maude, was*
*the daughter of pioneer*
*L.W. Burkhardt. Their son*
*Ralph was born in 1908.* ■

Carl Kettler came to the theater as a child, playing minor parts with the great actor Joseph Jefferson. His father was the actor's private secretary for 15 years. The train carrying Kettler and his family pulled into town on Nov. 12, 1901, he recalled in 1964.

In October 1908, he opened the Bijou, West Palm Beach's first theater, in Jefferson's building on Clematis Street. The first feature was *The Great Train Robbery.*

He moved the Bijou to Narcissus and Clematis streets, and then replaced it with the grand Kettler Theatre in 1924. The $500,000 theater had 1,400 seats, colored lights, fans, and smoking rooms for men and was hailed as "the finest structure south of Atlanta."

Kettler's competition, the Arcade, opened in October 1927 on First Street and showed the city's first talkies. In 1929 Kettler would show the first color talkie.

The Kettler later became The Palms. It was razed in 1965.

BEST PLACE TO GO ON SATURDAY NIGHT, MID-1920S
*Going to the Kettler was a thrill for locals like T.T. Reese Jr., who recalls, "Every Saturday night, we'd take the ferry over to Carl Kettler's theater to see* The Perils of Pauline. *My mama made me put on shoes, and I'd always say, "Ah, Mama, but Mr. Kettler's got those fuzzy rugs in the balcony, and I want to get my feet on those fuzzy rugs."* ■

# Sun Dance: Downtown's fanciest festival

### INDIANS, BABIES AND LOTS AND LOTS OF CREPE PAPER

*From 1916 to 1950, no March was complete without the Seminole Sun Dance, a three-day festival that brought everyone downtown. "Barco Motors (then on Third Street between Dixie and the F.E.C. tracks) donated cars, which were decorated with crepe paper. High school students rode in and on the cars, and each year, a king and queen were featured in the parade," remembers Helen Hopkins Ryan, who came to West Palm Beach in 1928. Seminoles performed sun-worshiping ceremonies, residents dressed in Seminole costumes, and there was even a baby contest (above in 1917). Below, City Park decorated for an early Sun Dance.* ◼

## The high schools

# Tops in their class

"The panorama of names and faces pass
on into the dimness . . .
a sigh, perhaps a tear, for days
that we can never recall.
Then a smile for the memories,
foolish, sad and sweet,
all entangled in our carefree youth —
adieu and farewell!"

From Palm Beach High School's
1935 yearbook, *The Royal Palm.*

# The high schools

## Palm Beach High
### 1908-1970

## Industrial High
### 1917-1950

## Roosevelt High
### 1950-1970

*PREVIOUS PAGES:*
*PALM BEACH HIGH*
*TREASURES*
*Assembled around Judy*
*Watson's (Class of '57)*
*"Wildcats" sweater is*
*memorabilia from several*
*years: the baseball trophy*
*won by the district champs*
*of 1938 (the team went on*
*to be state champs and*
*"champions of Dixie,"*
*beating Georgia and North*
*and South Carolina), a*
*photo of the 1941 band at*
*the U.S. Capitol after per-*
*forming in the cherry blos-*
*som parade, a band*
*plaque, some fraternity/*
*sorority pins, a tile of the*
*Palm Beach High crest*
*made in 1947, the 1933*
*issue of the yearbook, The*
*Royal Palm, and photos of*
*the Central School around*
*1910 and the girls' basket-*
*ball team, 1912.* ■

*Palm Beach High School, 1932.* ■

They were so much more than buildings and books. West Palm Beach's original high schools were the heart of the city.

"The school was really a definitive part of the community," said Dr. Reginald Stambaugh, who graduated from Palm Beach High in 1947. "People looked to the school to help them fill their social calendar."

This was true, too, for the first black high school, Industrial, which is now Palmview Elementary.

"Everybody knew everybody," said Bettye Tanner Dawson, who graduated with Industrial's last class, the Class of 1950. "There was a lot of culture — band concerts, choral concerts, the plays."

Palm Beach High began as Central School in 1908, when West Palm Beach had outgrown the little four-room schoolhouse at Clematis and Dixie. It rose "on the hill" at Hibiscus and Sapodilla — in the middle of wilderness.

Some children walked up the dirt road to school; others were picked up by horse-drawn wagon. They all piled into the single building — with its distinctive tower (knocked down in the '28 hurricane) — that housed all grades. By 1922, there were three school buildings on the hill: Central Junior High just south of the original building, which became the elementary school, and Palm Beach High to the north.

Roosevelt High School, at 15th and Tamarind, was an outgrowth of Industrial. It used the same song and mascot — the Maroon Devil.

And some rituals were the same, such as the respect shown to upperclassmen, Dawson remembered.

"At Industrial, we used to have to line up on the court every morning, class by class, and say the pledge before marching off to our classes. There was a big shade tree with a water fountain under it and benches — and that was the hallowed ground. It belonged to the seniors. You looked forward to your day when you were a senior and could stand under that tree."

At Palm Beach High, the sitting spot was "the wall" — the 2-foot-high wall around campus where students ate lunch and hung out.

It's just one of the millions of memories for the kids — now well-grown — of West Palm Beach's first high schools.

"I used to think I was being overly sentimental to care so much about Palm Beach High," said Bobby Riggs, president of the Class of '43, custodian of the Palm Beach High Museum on Flagler Drive. "But just the other day, a classmate came in and found a high school photograph of her brother, who had just passed away. And she sat down and cried and cried.

"The place meant so much to so many people."

*1956 MAJORETTES*
*From Roosevelt High*
*School.* ■

*SCHOOL HYMN*
*Roosevelt High School's song was written by the choral director, Maria Gilliam. "Mrs. Gilliam and Mr. (Leander) Kirksey, the band leader, brought music to the kids," Bettye Dawson remembers. "They called Mr. Kirksey 'Chief,' and his kids adore him to this day."* ■

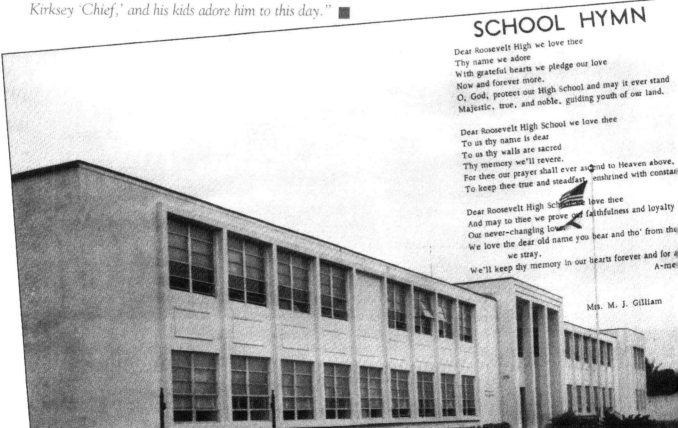

## SCHOOL HYMN

Dear Roosevelt High we love thee
Thy name we adore
With grateful hearts we pledge our love
Now and forever more.
O, God, protect our High School and may it ever stand
Majestic, true, and noble, guiding youth of our land.

Dear Roosevelt High School we love thee
To us thy name is dear
To us thy walls are sacred
Thy memory we'll revere.
For thee our prayer shall ever ascend to Heaven above,
To keep thee true and steadfast, enshrined with constan[t]

Dear Roosevelt High School we love thee
And may to thee we prove our faithfulness and loyalty
Our never-changing love.
We love the dear old name you bear and tho' from the[e]
we stray,
We'll keep thy memory in our hearts forever and for a[ye]
A-me[n]

Mrs. M. J. Gilliam

CRACKER'S
DYNASTY
Cracker Johnson,
parked on Banyan
Street between
Rosemary and the
railroad tracks, in the
black business dis-
trict. The building on
the right is the pool
room and cafe run by
David M. Shannon
Jr. Note the sign on
Johnson's car — it is
the same "West Palm
Beach" sign shown
on Page 97. ■

# Cracker Johnson: Tycoon of the black community

Cracker Johnson was both the king of the city's black neighborhoods and its Robin Hood.

A son of a mixed marriage — he earned his nickname because he could pass as white — James J. Johnson worked as a cabin boy, sponge diver, steamship captain, and eventually a deputy sheriff in Key West. Sent to West Palm Beach in 1912 to look for a prisoner, he liked the place so much he went back to Key West without his man, quit, and returned.

Johnson bought a building on Banyan Street; a rooming house upstairs, pool tables downstairs. Climbing aboard the real estate boom, he built a movie the-ater — the Dixie, on Rosemary and Third Street — homes and rental opera-tions and bought other property across the state. He opened the Florida Bar and helped found a club for "colored gentlemen."

Many blacks couldn't borrow money from white-owned banks, so they bor-rowed from Johnson.

He also reportedly smuggled liquor during Prohibition and was wildly suc-cessful running the "bolita" numbers game, conducting both local games and the Cuban bolita. Johnson was reportedly raking in up to $10,000 a week by the 1940s.

One of his top aides was the father of Robbie Littles, who would become a city commissioner. Another was Joe Orr, whose son would become an associate schools superintendent.

Cracker Johnson was fatally shot on July 2, 1946 — he had rushed to Orr's aid in an attack behind Johnson's bar. One of the two attackers, who were brothers, was killed and the other was later captured. At Johnson's funeral, hun-dreds of people — black and white — fought for a standing-room-only spot.

# The Ashley gang:
# South Florida's most notorious criminals

The Ashley gang terrorized South Florida during the 1910s and the Roaring '20s.

John Ashley was the eldest of five sons of a wood chopper for Flagler's railroad who had settled in West Palm Beach. John was only 18 in 1911 when he was suspected in the slaying of a Seminole trader. He ran off two deputies, and told Sheriff George Baker not to send chicken-hearted men after him. It was the beginning of a 13-year feud.

After three years on the lam, Ashley returned to South Florida and, only one day into the murder trial, bolted a 10-foot fence and escaped the Palm Beach County jail.

Ashley and an accomplice robbed a train, then a bank in Stuart, where Ashley was captured after his pal accidentally shot him in the eye.

The murder charges were eventually dropped and Ashley went to the state prison for 17 years in the Stuart robbery. Two years later he walked away from a road gang. For the next three years, he ran rum from the Bahamas. One night, as two brothers were returning from the Bahamas, Ashley dreamed they were caught in a storm. They were never seen again.

Ashley was caught — again — in 1921, but escaped state prison — again — three years later. During his stay, his nephew had robbed a Stuart bank, cleverly dressed as a woman. After his escape, John and his gang robbed a Pompano Beach bank, and Ashley left a bullet as a gift for his good friend, Sheriff Bob Baker, who had succeeded his father George as sheriff.

The next move was Baker's. He raided Ashley's still in Martin County; Ashley killed Deputy Fred Baker — identified as the sheriff's cousin — while a deputy shot Ashley's father.

Ashley's luck ran out the night after Halloween in 1924. He and three partners were stopped on a bridge near Sebastian. Moments later, all four were dead, face down on the bridge.

While two bystanders said later the gangsters stood cuffed on the bridge, the cops insisted the gangsters had pulled guns on them.

A judge agreed, and few wept for the Ashleys save their mother, who buried a husband and four of her five sons, all dead of the violent lifestyle they had led.

*THE GANGSTER*
*John Ashley, who lost an eye in a robbery, was public enemy No. 1.* ∎

*THE SHERIFF*
*Robert C. Baker, who brought the Ashleys to the ultimate justice.* ∎

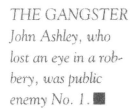

$500- REWARD -$500
I will pay a reward of Five Hundred Dollars for information leading to the capture and conviction of John Ashley, dead or alive, slayer of Fred A. Baker, Deputy Sheriff.
FRANK J BAKER,
319 Fern St.

*THE PRICE OF VIOLENCE*
*Ad in a 1924 issue of* The Palm Beach Post. *Deputy Sheriff Fred Baker was one of Ashley's victims.* ∎

# Bathing beauties

In the earliest days of Palm Beach bathing, a beach censor had to OK a woman's swimsuit before she stepped onto the beach. "The censor determined if her hose were dark enough so it didn't look like she was bare-legged," says historian Jim Ponce. The rules had been relaxed slightly by the time this woman (below) lounged near Gus' Baths ("all wend their paths to Gus' Baths" says the back of the photograph). At right: "The Palm Beach Smile was noted on the pretty face of Mrs. Gene Gordon Culver of Chicago as she appeared for her morning dip," says this Royal Poinciana Hotel photo from 1925 (top). An anonymous bather poses for a postcard (below). ■

## "COWBOY OF THE SEA"

Gus Jordahn was one of the most colorful men in Palm Beach. He owned Gus' Baths, a swimming complex with two pools and steam cabinets around the corner from Worth Avenue on South Ocean Boulevard. He was famous for capturing and riding loggerhead turtles — and for saving foundering bathers in the ocean in front of Gus' Baths. It is said that he saved 300 lives through the years. He also rescued small boats by swimming out to them when he spotted trouble. On his 50th birthday, he swam across Lake Worth and back. Across the front of his building was a huge sign, "Welcome to Our Ocean." ■

*Above, Clematis Street in the early '20s. Right, another version of the "West Palm Beach" sign adorns this Buick, parked on Olive Avenue at First Street in the late '20s. Note the sign for the Willys-Knight garage on Olive.* ■

# Honk if you love West Palm Beach

Henry Ford's Model T came out in 1908, and in the early years of motor travel, "the passing of an automobile was such an event we housewives would leave our dishes unwashed to go stand on the front porch and gape," said Mrs. E.E. Geer, who arrived in 1894.

By 1913 there were so many cars in West Palm Beach that motorists were required to buy license tags for the first time. (This prompted Franklin Sheen, who had one of the first cars in town, to retort, "What will happen next? They'll be charging us for the air we breathe!")

And by the '20s, all types of "wheels" filled Clematis Street — Afromobiles, bicycles and motorcars, all parked in the center of the street.

Edward J. Maas, whose father managed the Salt Air Hotel, remembers his early days behind the wheel this way:

"The first time I ever went 60 was in a Stutz Bearcat headed south on Dixie Highway toward Lake Worth. Dodge cars, with their distinctive gear shift pattern, were popular because they reputedly 'pulled sand' well.

"By 1926 the roads were in good shape for sustained travel. I remember a driver who bragged about making it from Jacksonville in one day."

## EARLY BUMPER STICKERS

*"This sign dates from at least as far back as 1926, possibly a year or so earlier," says its owner, Edward Maas. "It was on the front of our 1925 Willys-Knight six-cylinder Victoria coupe when we drove north one summer to Cincinnati, New Jersey and New York. Going northbound in Tennessee, we saw an oncoming car with the same sign, and we both beeped our horns. This was a big deal! My mother kept the sign for 50 years, until she died in Asbury Park, N.J., in 1976. She loved West Palm Beach."* ■

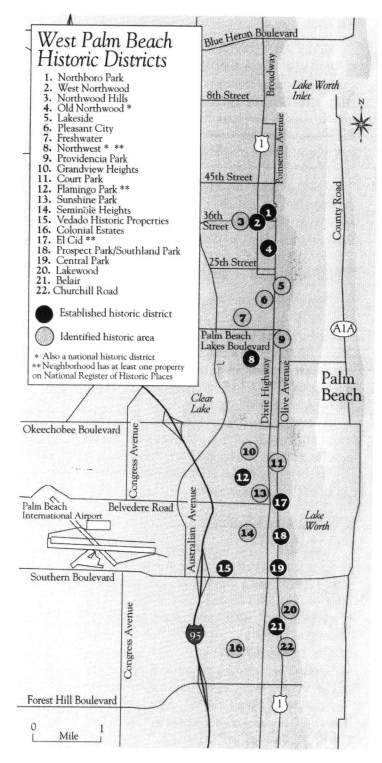

## Chapter 5

# Birth of the First Neighborhoods

*By Ava Van de Water*
*Photography by C.J. Walker*

In the early days, only a few cabins dotted the western shores of Lake Worth. Settlers lived off the land, and pineapples were a favorite crop.

But when Henry Flagler brought his hotel workers to town, West Palm Beach's first neighborhoods were born. And by the time the great Florida land boom of the '20s had busted, dozens of neighborhoods had developed.

The black community settled in Northwest, Pleasant City and Freshwater. Bankers and businesspeople flocked to Intracoastal neighborhoods such as El Cid and Southland/Prospect Park.

And since the real estate boom came at the height of Prohibition — 1920 to 1933 — some neighborhoods, such as Providencia Park, became home to bootleggers.

Here's a look at how the city's historic neighborhoods developed — and the people who developed them.

GRAND WELCOME
*An entryway in El Cid, one of West Palm Beach's boom neighborhoods.* ■

### West Palm Beach Historic Districts

1. Northboro Park
2. West Northwood
3. Northwood Hills
4. Old Northwood *
5. Lakeside
6. Pleasant City
7. Freshwater
8. Northwest * **
9. Providencia Park
10. Grandview Heights
11. Court Park
12. Flamingo Park **
13. Sunshine Park
14. Seminole Heights
15. Vedado Historic Properties
16. Colonial Estates
17. El Cid **
18. Prospect Park/Southland Park
19. Central Park
20. Lakewood
21. Belair
22. Churchill Road

● Established historic district

○ Identified historic area

\* Also a national historic district
\*\* Neighborhood has at least one property on National Register of Historic Places

# Guide to architectural styles

## Mission

West Palm Beach's most common architectural style. There are almost 2,000 mission-style houses and buildings in the city, mostly built from 1920 to 1925. Mission homes feature smooth or textured stucco walls, minimal decoration, flat roofs with widely overhanging eaves and porch roofs supported by large square piers.

Most of the houses on Avon Road between Florida and Georgia avenues are mission style. The home shown is on Murray Road in the Lakewood district.

## Mediterranean revival

The second-most common style in the city (about 400), inspired by society architect Addison Mizner's elaborate Palm Beach mansions. Mostly built in the boom of the 1920s, these feature asymmetrical shapes with pastel stucco walls, barrel-tile roofs, balconies, decorative accents and loggias.

There are good examples throughout the city, but especially on Lakewood Road between Flagler Drive and Olive Avenue. The home shown is in the 200 block of Barcelona in the El Cid neighborhood.

## Craftsman bungalow

Literally, a low house with porches. In 1915, about 75 percent of the houses in West Palm Beach were bungalows. The modest one-story buildings were built with natural materials (brick, stone, limestone, stucco and rusticated block), and have low-pitched gabled roofs and porches.

There are some examples of this style throughout the city, but especially in the Northwest and Grandview Heights neighborhoods. The home shown is at 28th and Spruce in Northwood.

$M$any architectural styles appear in West Palm Beach's boom-era homes, but these are the most common and most distinctive.

### Frame vernacular

Along with bungalows, this is the city's oldest style, built from 1895 to 1915. A revolt against Victorian style, the frame vernacular house has simple lines. It is typically rectangular and mounted on masonry piers for air circulation. Roofs are normally shingled and steeply pitched. Eaves extend over the house for weather protection and attic dormers provide ventilation.

This style can be found throughout the city. The home shown is on 28th Street in Northwood.

### Shingle style

Noted for its plain, wooden shingled roofs and walls, this style was popular from the 1880s to about 1910. Most had verandas and simple ornamental details. The open floorplan drew from Queen Anne, vernacular colonial and colonial revival styles. There are two excellent examples of this style: 200 Pershing Way (shown here, one of the oldest homes in the El Cid neighborhood) and 201 Monceaux Road.

### Shotgun

A type of frame vernacular built from 1895 to 1915, this style is a one-story rectangular house with front gabled roof. Usually built in rows on small lots, this style gets its name from the floor plan — a hall goes from the front door to the back. If you were to fire a shotgun from the front door, it would go out the back without hitting a wall. Common housing for black workers, there are few examples left in the city. The building shown is in the Northwest neighborhood.

# The neighborhoods

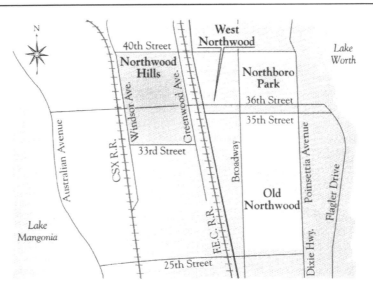

## Old Northwood

Old Northwood was developed from 1920 to 1927 — the height of the city's real estate boom. The Pinewood Development Co., whose partners were David F. Dunkle, Orrin Randolph and G.W. Bingham, platted and developed the area, most of which had been owned by the Rev. Elbridge Gale.

Gale, a professor of horticulture, settled here in 1884. He grew tasty Haden mangoes on the property, but later his son converted the land to a poultry farm. Gale's cabin, built around 1888, was one of the first built on the west side of Lake Worth, on what is now the middle of 29th Street and Poinsettia Avenue. Later the cabin was moved, and it is believed the house at 401 29th St. was built around that cabin, somewhere between 1900 and 1910.

Old Northwood became a neighborhood of what was considered extravagant Mediterranean revival, mission and frame vernacular houses, at $30,000 to $36,000. The buyers were professionals, entrepreneurs and tradesmen. Among them was Dunkle, who was mayor of West Palm Beach.

There are houses here designed by notable architects John Volk (best known for his Palm Beach houses), William Manly King (who designed Palm Beach High School and the Armory Arts Center) and Henry Steven Harvey (whose Seaboard Railroad Passenger Station on Tamarind Avenue is listed in the National Register of Historic Places).

The neighborhood became a West Palm Beach historic district in 1991 and a national historic district in June 1994.

GALE HOUSE
*This house at 401 29th St. was probably built around the cabin of the Rev. Elbridge Gale, sometime between 1900 and 1910.* ■

## Northboro Park

An expansion of Old Northwood, Northboro Park was mostly custom houses for upper-middle-class professionals. Most of the houses are Mediterranean revival, mission and frame vernacular.

Developed from 1923 to 1940, the neighborhood became the city's second historic district (November 1992) and the historic designation may soon expand north to 45th Street.

The oldest building in the neighborhood is Northboro Elementary School at 36th Street and Spruce, built in 1925 by DaCamara and Chace. The first home in Northboro Park is 418 36th St., built in 1923.

## West Northwood

Cashing in on the real estate boom, developers of West Northwood built speculative and custom houses for upper-middle-class professionals from 1925 to '27. Major developers were DaCamara and Chace, H.E. Rise and J.C. Griswell, and dominant architectural styles are Mediterranean revival and mission.

Although the area was declining, that has reversed in recent years, as more investors buy and restore the houses.

West Northwood became a city historic district in August 1993.

## Northwood Hills

Folklore has it that this was the neighborhood of 1920s pirates who smuggled rum and other liquor during Prohibition. The high ridge and tall houses (especially the "castle" houses on Eastview and Westview roads) provided owners an unobstructed view of the inlet.

Recently, residents have fought to maintain the character of the neighborhood, which was developed from 1926 to '28 and has many examples of Mediterranean revival and masonry vernacular houses.

*CASTLE LORE*

*There are four "castle" houses in Northwood Hills, but the most elaborate is at 3509 Eastview Ave. The three-story Mediterranean revival house has a castle tower, and from the third floor, you can see the Intracoastal Waterway several miles away. Legend has it that bootleggers built the house to see their rum-laden ships entering the port during Prohibition, but the truth may be less colorful (one version is the house was built for a retired New York tax collector).* ∎

**RESTORED TO GLORY**

*Raleigh Hill and Colin Rayner restored Hibiscus House and turned it into a bed and breakfast. They also started the Old Northwood Neighborhood Association to preserve the historic homes.* ■

# Hibiscus House

In 1922, Old Northwood was being transformed from mango groves to a bustling neighborhood — largely because of David F. Dunkle, then mayor of West Palm Beach and head of Pinewood Development Co.

Dunkle built an impressive frame vernacular house on the northwest corner of 30th Street and Spruce Avenue.

But by the 1980s, the house had fallen into disrepair, reflecting the neighborhood's decline. Revived in 1986 by antiques dealer and interior designer Raleigh Hill and former Toronto schoolteacher Colin Rayner, the house is now one of six historically significant homes in Old Northwood.

**A MIX OF ANTIQUE TREASURES**

*French doors on either side of the fireplace are typical of frame vernacular houses of this period (above). In the dining room (right), an oak buffet and dining table date from the late 1880s.* ■

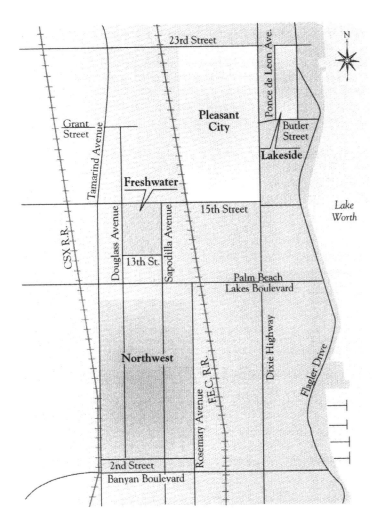

23rd Street

Pleasant City

Ponce de Leon Ave.

Butler Street

Lakeside

Grant Street

Tamarind Avenue

Freshwater

Lake Worth

15th Street

Douglass Avenue

Sapodilla Avenue

13th St.

CSX R.R.

Palm Beach Lakes Boulevard

Northwest

Rosemary Avenue

F.E.C. R.R.

Dixie Highway

Flagler Drive

2nd Street

Banyan Boulevard

N

## Lakeside

This neighborhood of shingle-style frame vernacular houses was developed in the early 1900s, before the real estate boom. It now consists mostly of apartments and commercial buildings.

## Pleasant City

Built for blacks who worked in Henry Flagler's Palm Beach, Pleasant City was established in 1905 but not incorporated into the city limits until 1912.

Although rich in history, the neighborhood of mostly frame vernacular houses has deteriorated, plagued by bad zoning decisions, poor construction and years of neglect. Its street names reflect better times: Beautiful, Contentment, Comfort.

## Freshwater

Developed as a neighborhood for West Palm Beach's wealthy blacks from 1914 to 1923, Freshwater featured grander houses than in the neighboring Northwest area. Most buildings were constructed by local black builders and contractors. Hazel Augustus, West Palm Beach's first black architect, designed many of the houses and churches. And builder Simeon Mather constructed many of the homes. There are many good examples of frame vernacular architecture here.

## Northwest

West Palm Beach's first historic district to be included on the National Register of Historic Places (February 1992), the Northwest neighborhood was first settled in 1894, when the black community was moved from the Styx in Palm Beach to West Palm Beach. It also served as the city's segregated black community from 1929 to 1960 (along with Pleasant City).

Northwest remains a predominantly black community but according to the city planning department, most middle- and upper-class blacks moved to other neighborhoods after desegregation. Tamarind and Rosemary avenues were the commercial centers for blacks by 1915, but most commercial buildings have been demolished or remodeled so the architecture is no longer significant.

There are still good examples of late 19th- and early 20th-century American bungalow/craftsman-style homes in this neighborhood, which also has mission, shotgun, Bahamian vernacular and American Foursquare styles.

The Alice Frederick Mickens house, at 801 Fourth St., is listed on the National Register of Historic Places. Mickens was a philanthropist and humanitarian who promoted education for black youth (see Chapter 3).

Another notable house is the Gwen Cherry house at 625 Division Ave. Cherry, Florida's first black woman legislator and a resident of Miami, inherited the house from relative Mollie Holt, who built the house in 1926. Now it is the Palm Beach County Black Historical Society.

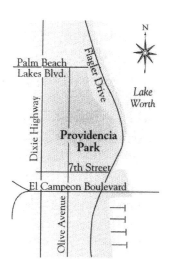

# Providencia Park

This small neighborhood, nestled between Good Samaritan Hospital and the Flagler Memorial Bridge, is named for the Spanish ship Providencia that ran aground in 1878 in Palm Beach with 20,000 coconuts.

E.M. Brelsford, an early settler and hardware store owner, owned most of the land along Eighth Street; and Sidney Maddock, owner of the Palm Beach Hotel, owned most of the land from Ninth Street to Good Samaritan Hospital. Businessman Marion Gruber and developer Bror J. Carlberg developed the area between 1920 and '27.

In 1919 lakefront lots along Flagler Drive sold for about $8,000 each and lots fronting Olive Avenue sold for about $3,000 each. The neighborhood had a feverish building pace in the early '20s, ahead of the peak boom period. Many current residents are descendants of the original developers and landowners, many of whom worked on Henry Flagler's railroad.

Developed at the beginning of Prohibition, the neighborhood also had its share of bootleggers. Zada Rogerson, who has lived in a 1924 house on North Olive Avenue all her life, said her father used to help dig trenches at night to bury rum alongside the houses.

The most dominant architectural styles are Mediterranean revival and colonial revival, but you'll also see many ranch-style houses that were built after World War II.

Okeechobee Boulevard

Acacia Road

Court Park

Lake Worth

Flamingo Drive

El Cid

Dixie Highway

Flagler Drive

Monceaux Rd.

Prospect Park/ Southland Park

Washington Road

Monroe Drive

Wenonah Place

Central Park

Flagler Drive

Southern Boulevard

# Court Park

Court Park is a general name given to a number of small subdivisions that originally were 3- to 5-acre estates. Although no estate homes remain, some of the oldest houses in the city are here, including the home of West Palm Beach's first mayor, John S. Earman. Earman's brown shingle house still stands at 12 Currie Crescent — just north of the Norton Gallery of Art, between Memorial Presbyterian Church at 1300 S. Olive Ave. and the office building at 1311 S. Flagler Drive.

While there still are prairie-style, masonry and wood-frame vernacular homes in Court Park, the neighborhood — developed in the early 1920s — is now dominated by condominiums, Palm Beach Atlantic College and the expanding Norton Gallery of Art.

# Prospect Park/Southland Park

Promoted as a high-end neighborhood patterned after the prominent Prospect Park district in Brooklyn, this area consisted of mostly smaller estates for prominent businesspeople and northern investors. It was developed from 1920 to 1935 and became a city historic district in November 1993. Notable architects William Manly King and Belford Shoumate designed houses in the neighborhood, which has a concentration of Mediterranean revival and mission revival houses.

# Central Park

Central Park is a collective name for several subdivisions north of Southern Boulevard. It originally was part of the Estates of South Palm Beach (which went from Wenonah Place to Pilgrim Road east of Dixie Highway).

Like other West Palm Beach neighborhoods, the Estates of South Palm Beach boomed after Henry Flagler's descent on Palm Beach. However, the idea for the village was conceived years before Flagler's first visit to the area. In 1884, James W. Copp, a bachelor in the boating business, borrowed $367.20 from Valentine Jones (a single woman from Rhode Island) to buy the land.

The ownership of what is now known as Central Park changed hands many times before being developed. Around 1919, the tropical wilderness was transformed into an exclusive neighborhood with curbed roads, sidewalks and a pier (at the foot of what is now Southern Boulevard).

The neighborhood became part of West Palm Beach in 1926, and was named a city historic district in December 1993.

## HOME OF FIRST MAYOR

*The brown shingle house of West Palm Beach's first mayor, John Earman, still stands at 12 Currie Crescent, just north of the Norton Gallery of Art.* ■

## CHARMING PROSPECT PARK

*Details from a home on Marlborough Road in Prospect Park. The neighborhood, which features some winding streets, was developed from 1920 to 1935.* ■

# El Cid

ART DECO
*The Ralph Wagner house on South Flagler Drive in El Cid was designed in Art Deco style by Belford Shoumate.* ■

Noted for its Mediterranean revival and mission-style homes, El Cid developed in the height of Florida's real estate boom.

It quickly became one of the most upscale residential areas in the city, with many houses designed by prominent architects, including Maurice Fatio, Belford Shoumate, William Manly King, and Harvey and Clarke.

In the late 1800s, most of the land north of Sunset Road was pineapple fields, but the crop dwindled (due to disease and stiff competition from Cuba) in the early 1900s. Pittsburgh socialite Jay Phipps (son of Andrew Carnegie's partner in U.S. Steel) subdivided the old pineapple fields in the 1920s. He named it El Cid, after the celebrated Spanish hero, Rodrigo Diaz de Bivar, who conquered Valencia in 1094. He was called "Cid," meaning "lord."

El Cid attracted affluent residents who were prominent in the city's history. One notable resident was Circuit Judge C.E. Chillingworth, murdered in 1955 in a conspiracy masterminded by then-Municipal Court Judge Joseph Peel (see Chapter 9). The home of Ralph and Ann Norton (he founded the Norton Gallery of Art) at 253 Barcelona Road is on the National Register of Historic Places.

One of the oldest houses in the neighborhood is the Christian Kirk house at 200 Pershing Way, built in 1909 (photograph on Page 101). Kirk was a Danish carpenter who moved here to help build Flagler's properties (he did most of the trim work in the Flagler Museum). Kirk, whose family still owns the house, bought what is now known as Pershing Way from pioneer William Lanehart. During the Depression, Kirk subdivided the land and sold off the lakefront property. A mule team moved the Kirk house, which once faced the lake, from what is now the middle of Pershing Way and turned it to face north.

El Cid became a city historic district in June 1993.

# Honchar House

Neglected for years, the house at 218 Valencia Road in West Palm Beach's El Cid neighborhood was an eyesore — until Bob and Nancy Honchar bought it in 1990.

They spent two years restoring the 1925 Mediterranean-revival house, removing bastard additions and sandblasting paint off pecky cypress ceilings.

The Honchars maintained the original roof line and original windows where possible but added a narrow, two-story addition, changing the small formal structure into a four-bedroom, 3 1/2-bath home.

Their efforts won them West Palm Beach's first historic preservation award in November 1993.

*REVEALING THE CEILING*
*The Honchars sandblasted the ceiling to uncover the original pecky cypress, then added decorative columns.* ■

*WINNER OF WEST PALM BEACH'S FIRST HISTORIC PRESERVATION AWARD*
*It took two years for Bob and Nancy Honchar to restore the 1925 Mediterranean revival home. The upstairs addition includes wrought iron balcony and French doors. Most dramatic is the hooded plaster fireplace in the living room (next pages).* ■

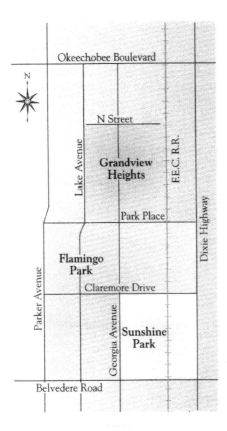

# Grandview Heights

One of the city's oldest neighborhoods still intact, Grandview Heights was built as an extension of Palm Beach Heights from around 1910 to 1925.

Almost all of Palm Beach Heights and half of Grandview Heights was demolished in 1989 to make way for the proposed Downtown/Uptown project, which remains undeveloped.

Grandview Heights originally attracted construction workers who helped build the luxury hotels, ministers and store owners.

In recent years, residents rallied to stop random demolition of neighborhood homes. And they banded together to chase drug dealers and prostitutes from the neighborhood. New investors are helping bring back the neighborhood, which has one of the city's best collection of early craftsman-style bungalows, as well as some modest, Mediterranean revival-style homes.

# Flamingo Park

Originally a pineapple plantation, Flamingo Park was established by local contractors and developers (such as Hansell Hall, James Ebert, Clare Warner and Edward Roddy), who saw the potential in this area — one of the highest coastal ridge sections from downtown West Palm Beach to Miami. Some ridge houses even had ocean views from upper floors.

Houses cost about $10,000 to $18,000 in the boom era, and many buyers were owners of shops and businesses on fashionable Dixie Highway nearby. Recently, residents rallied to have stop signs installed throughout the neighborhood and have banded together to ward off commercial and industrial zoning. Property values are rising as residents renovate and restore Spanish-style houses.

Most of the homes in the neighborhood, developed from 1921 to 1930, are mission style, but nearly every style is represented. There are many Mediterranean revival-style houses along the high ridge line.

Only two buildings in the historic district are known to have been designed by architects: 701 Flamingo Drive designed by Harvey and Clarke, and the Armory Arts Center designed by William Manly King.

The neighborhood became a West Palm Beach historic district in January 1994.

# Sunshine Park

Originally considered part of Flamingo Park (it is actually the missing southeast corner of the otherwise square boundaries of Flamingo Park), the 1920s neighborhood attracted middle-income residents who bought smaller houses on the 40- to 50-foot lots. Most of the houses are mission-style. There are some streets, such as Avon Road between Florida and Georgia avenues, where every house is mission-style.

# Seminole Heights

Although most houses built in the boom 1920s were influenced by Spanish styles, it is interesting that this three-street area is called Seminole Heights and the streets have Indian names. Today the frame vernacular houses are sandwiched between 1940s housing.

# Vedado Historic Properties

Platted by the Suburban Developers Co. in 1924, the area developed over the next 11 years as a prominent, independent residential area with its own water source and a park as its centerpiece. Streets have mostly Spanish names and the mostly mission and Mediterranean revival-style homes exhibit a Spanish influence.

The area north of the neighborhood is vacant — it was the Hillcrest neighborhood where most homes were leveled (some were moved to other neighborhoods) because of airport noise.

Vedado became a West Palm Beach historic district in January 1994.

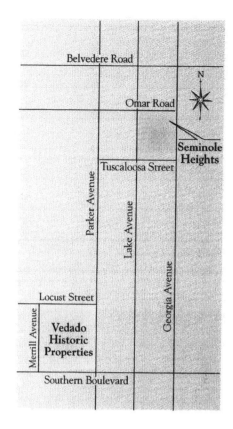

## Lakewood

Developed the same time as nearby Belair (1924 to '26), this neighborhood originally was a large estate. It may have been a pineapple plantation that was later subdivided. There are some beautiful examples of Mediterranean revival and mission architecture.

## Belair

Developed from 1925 to 1935 as a neighborhood for tradesmen and real estate salesmen who helped develop Palm Beach County, some of Belair was originally a pineapple plantation owned by Richard Hone.

Hone's frame vernacular house, built around 1895, still stands at 211 Plymouth Road.

After Hone was murdered in 1902, his property was sold to George Currie, who created Currie Development Co. But before it was developed, the land was sold to William Ohlhaber, who raised coconut palms and ferns.

Eventually Ohlhaber platted the subdivision and sold off lots. The first house built in the subdivision was Ohlhaber's mission-style home at 205 Pilgrim. Ohlhaber's grandson said Ohlhaber bought the tract to provide dockage for his 90-foot yacht, but the yacht ran aground in the Gulf of Mexico and never reached Lake Worth.

In 1947 Hone's house was bought by Max Brombacher, Henry Flagler's chief engineer, and it remains in the Brombacher family today.

Belair became West Palm Beach's fourth historic district in August 1993.

## Churchill Road

This south-end neighborhood was sparsely developed in the mid-1920s. Dominating the small district are the Mediterranean revival house at 124 Churchill (built in 1925) and a Georgian revival home at 101 Churchill, designed by prominent architect John Volk for a shipping executive in 1940.

*MEDITERRANEAN REVIVAL BEAUTY*
*The house at 124 Churchill Road was built in 1925.*
*This is the entry hall, decorated for the 1994 Red*
*Cross Designer Showhouse.* ▪

*IN BELAIR*
*Part of the Belair neighborhood was originally a pineapple plantation owned by Richard Hone. Hone's frame vernacular house, built around 1895, still stands at 211 Plymouth Road.* ■

## Colonial Estates

Actually nine separate subdivisions, this area developed as a middle-income residential area in the 1920s to 1935. Roughly from Southern to Forest Hill boulevards, from just west of Dixie Highway to Lake Avenue, it had a second development boom in the 1940s. The neighborhood consists of mostly one-story mission-style houses, but there are some frame vernacular and a few Mediterranean revival styles as well.

Residents in the early days were mostly the managerial staffs for large Palm Beach estates — butlers, housekeepers, chauffeurs. It is said that society architect Addison Mizner's chauffeur lived on Garden Avenue. Most of the area — like most land south of Southern Boulevard — was platted by Alfred H. Wagg, but it was developed by others after Wagg went bankrupt during the Great Depression.

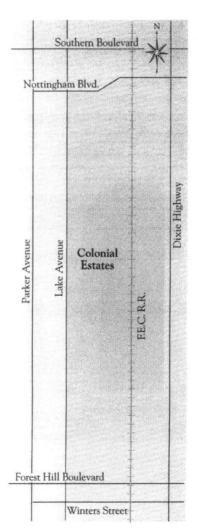

# Special entries

■ On 32nd Street, in Northwood

■ On Washington Road,
in Prospect Park

■ On Sunset Road,
in Flamingo Park

■ On Lakewood Road

■ On Valencia Road, in El Cid

## RUN ON THE FARMER'S BANK, 1926

*The corner of Olive Avenue and Clematis Street is packed with people trying to get their money out of the bank. By 1933, more than 200 Florida banks had closed, some of them in West Palm Beach. During the city's toughest times, West Palm Beach could not meet its payroll and resorted to paying employees in scrip. The city would write what amounted to IOUs for employees' landlords, grocers, utility companies, and other creditors. Some businesses took it; some didn't.* ■

## POSITIVE THINKING, 1928

*A group called the "Believers in West Palm Beach" produced a booklet on the assets and attributes of the city in 1928, just before the '28 hurricane. These illustrations (right) were included. The booklet acknowledged the "stabilization" that occurred after the frenzied boom years — "The development was too big and too sudden to be controlled . . ." And it stressed the positive, claiming that West Palm Beach and Palm Beach County appeared to be "entering the springtime of a new era of development."* ■

### Chapter 6

# The Bust

## 1926-1941

*"A boom means something that is soon over with; West Palm Beach should keep on growing like this for years."*
— West Palm Beach building inspector Jonathan H. Brophy, 1922

It was hard to believe that the unprecedented and unfathomable boom would suffer a "readjustment."

But what was most surprising was how quickly and how hard everything fell. From the height of the boom, 1924 and 1925, things had started to sour even by 1926.

Why did the South Florida boom crash? The list is long.

Railroads and ships couldn't get building materials down in time. The law was catching up with the con artists and the tax man with the speculators. The nation's stock market was getting sick.

Northern bankers, investors and chambers of commerce — watching their money exit — retaliated with negative campaigns that pointed out swindles or gouging or little weather problems called hurricanes.

Nervous speculators, in a bit of self-fulfilling prophecy, began to take the money and run. Then came the killer hurricanes of 1926 and 1928.

South Florida out-speculated its market, and demand began to drop.

When you're selling confidence, and the confidence departs, it's all over.

As late as 1929, the city had posted a boom-high total property value of $89 million, one and a half times the figure for just two years earlier. But it was all on paper, and it didn't take long for the real financial picture to catch up.

In one awful year, from 1929 to 1930, West Palm Beach's total property value dropped more than half. By 1935 it was down to a little more than its pre-boom 1920 value.

The city of gold hadn't just collapsed. It was rubble.

# Key events, 1926-1941

**1926:** Three West Palm Beach banks fail. One is Commercial Bank and Trust; its largest depositor, with $700,000, is city of West Palm Beach.

**March 1, 1926:** First synagogue, Temple Beth El, founded.

**April 1926:** Greenacres City incorporated. Disbanded in 1945 by Legislature amid financial woes; reincorporates 1946. (Town drops "City" in 1990.)

**June 1926:** Closing of Palm Beach Bank and Trust sparks run on area banks; by April 1930, 11 Palm Beach County banks will have failed.

**June 15, 1926:** City buys first city hall building, on Second Street between Dixie and Olive.

**Sept. 17, 1926:** Hurricane sweeps east coast; heavily damages Miami, killing 392, and hastens South Florida's real estate crash.

**Dec. 29, 1926:** The Breakers reopens with the famous twin towers.

**1927:** First full-scale sugar cane operation begins in Glades. Police department institutes traffic division.

**March 1927:** Nervous depositors make another run on area banks.

**May 11, 1927:** Delray Beach incorporated.

**June 12, 1927:** West Palm Beach's first business district south of downtown opens in Flamingo Park, along South Dixie Highway south of Okeechobee Boulevard.

**Jan 8, 1928:** Seaboard Coast Line's Orange Blossom Special makes first stop in West Palm Beach

**April 9, 1928:** Belle Glade incorporated.

*PALM BEACH AND WEST PALM BEACH, 1930*

*The Breakers had been rebuilt in 1926 after the 1925 fire, and the Royal Poinciana Hotel is a fraction of its former self. Part of the north wing and a center section were torn down after the 1928 hurricane. A greenhouse was built in the missing spot, and the domed slathouse stands today. A hotel was built onto Henry Flagler's Whitehall mansion.* ■

**Sept. 16, 1928:** Hurricane crumbles dike around Lake Okeechobee, drowning 1,800 to 3,000. Third-deadliest disaster in U.S. history.

**1929:** City's property value at boom high of $89 million. West Palm Beach acquires Connors Highway (what is now State Road 80 to Belle Glade and U.S. 98/441 around east shore of lake).

**1930:** Population: Florida 1,468,211; Palm Beach County 51,781, West Palm Beach 26,610. Property value plummets to $41.6 million.

**March 1930:** Last Palm Beach County Fair is held until after Depression.

**May 15, 1931:** Town of Boynton Beach incorporated. Changed name to Ocean Ridge in 1937; adjacent town of Boynton then became Boynton Beach.

**June 26, 1931:** Manalapan incorporated.

**Sept. 3, 1933:** Hurricane with 125 mph winds strikes between Jupiter and Fort Pierce, causing minimal damage to central Palm Beach County but extensive damage on the Treasure Coast.

**October 1933:** Palm Beach Junior College, first in state, opens.

**1934-35:** Royal Poinciana Hotel is razed.

**1935:** City's property value hits bottom at $18.2 million.

**Sept. 2, 1935:** Hurricane kills 409 and sweeps away the "Overseas Railroad" through the Keys.

**1936:** City refunds $20 million in bonds.

**July 31, 1936:** WJNO-AM 1230, area's first radio station, signs on at 1 p.m.

**Fall 1936:** Industrial High School football team earns state sports championship.

*PALM BEACH JUNIOR COLLEGE*
*The state's first public junior college began in 1933 at the old Palm Beach High School site with teachers from the next-door high school and 23 students.* ■

**Dec. 19, 1936:** New airport is dedicated; named Morrison Field in honor of secretary Grace K. Morrison.

**June 11, 1937:** Town of Golfview chartered.

**July 1, 1938:** Flagler Memorial Bridge, the furthest north of the three bridges between downtown West Palm Beach and Palm Beach, opens, replacing old wooden bridge.

**1939:** City again refunds bonds as financial problems continue.

**September 1939:** National Guard Armory opens at Howard Park, on Lake Street south of Okeechobee Boulevard.

**1940:** Population: Florida 1,897,414; Palm Beach County 79,989; West Palm Beach 33,693.

**Feb. 28, 1940:** Morrison Field leased to the U.S. Army for an air base.

**June 16, 1941:** South Bay incorporated.

# The great '28 hurricane:
## "The suffering is beyond words"

*IN RUINS*

*This pier (the Alba Hotel in Palm Beach is in the background) was just one casualty of the '28 hurricane. In West Palm Beach, 1,711 homes were destroyed and 6,363 homes were damaged. With its building on Banyan Street damaged (below), there was no "Today's News Today" for The Palm Beach Times.* ■

It was The Night 2,000 Died.

It might have been only 1,800. It might have been more than 3,000. Of America's natural disasters, only the Johnstown flood in 1889 and the Galveston hurricane of 1900 killed more people than drowned that night in the Glades.

The great storm of 1928 came ashore on Sunday, Sept. 16, at the Jupiter Lighthouse. The historic structure swayed a remarkable 17 inches as mortar squeezed from between bricks like toothpaste.

Damage estimates from Fort Pierce to Boca Raton surpassed $33 million in 1928 dollars — perhaps 10 times that in today's dollars. Downtown West Palm Beach was pummeled.

West Palm Beach resident M.A. Bishop wrote in a letter to his wife: "It is simply awful. I don't believe there are a dozen houses in town that aren't damaged."

County coroner T.M. Rickards said, "The street was shoulder-deep in debris. The suffering throughout is beyond words. Individual tales of horror, suffering and loss are numberless."

The storm then crossed Lake Okeechobee, a shallow frying-pan-shaped lake no more than 12 feet deep anywhere, and pushed water over the dike to pasture land north of the lake. When the eye passed and the winds shifted, all that water went roaring back into the lake, then crashed over the 5-

foot-high earth dike on the south shore and onto populated areas. Without the warning systems and evacuation methods taken for granted today, the pioneer farmers of the Glades were doomed.

Author Zora Neale Hurston wrote in her novel, *Their Eyes Were Watching God*: "It woke up old Okeechobee, and the monster began to roll in his bed."

Carmen Salvatore, then 32, abandoned his Pahokee lakefront home for fear it would come down. He, his wife and three children crossed 900 yards to a neighbor's house. It took an hour and 20 minutes.

Vernie Boots was 14, hiding in his family farmhouse near Lake Harbor. The house floated 100 yards before hitting high ground.

"It made two bounces. The house went down. Walls and everything came apart. Everybody went underwater."

The countryside stank with death. Bodies buried in the saturated muck popped out. Many were piled and burned. More than 1,600 were said to have gone into a mass grave on high ground at Port Mayaca.

Another 69 bodies were loaded on a barge and taken to a common grave at Woodlawn Cemetery in West Palm Beach. White bodies. About 674 blacks were said to have been buried in a pit that was lost to history, then rediscovered in 1991 behind a Tamarind Avenue home.

The 1928 hurricane — this region's "big one" — changed it forever. A 40-foot-high dike was built around the lake, the first in a series of dramatic alterations of nature to protect South Florida from floods.

CORPSES EVERYWHERE
*"Gov. John Martin counted 27 corpses floating in the water, and there were 126 dead along the road," read one account after the '28 storm. Some bodies were brought to West Palm Beach (above) — some were burned on the spot.* ■

# Grace Morrison: A persistent pilot

*FLYING BUFFS*
*Architect Maurice Fatio (back row, left) and his secretary, Grace Morrison (believed to be at right, center row) in their flying gear. Morrison (below) would be the driving force for West Palm Beach's first real airport.* ■

The driving force that led to the modern Palm Beach International Airport was an architect's secretary and weekend flier who never lived to see her dream fulfilled.

Although Wilbur Wright had come to town, looking for sites for a flying school, as far back as 1910, the closest thing to an airport in those pioneer years of aviation was a seaplane dock built just after World War I on the West Palm Beach lakefront north of the Flagler Bridge.

Later, attorney and former West Palm Beach Mayor R.D. Carmichael laid out a grass strip north of Belvedere Road and west of the Palm Beach Kennel Club for training pilots.

In the late 1920s, local businessmen, led by developer Cooper C. Lightbown, donated money for an airport between Belvedere Road and Southern Boulevard. "Lightbown Municipal Airport" was nothing more than a small strip with a windsock, an aerial beacon and a landing marker.

One of R.D. Carmichael's first students had been Grace K. Morrison, secretary, bookkeeper, and business manager to local architect Maurice Fatio. Morrison, who had come from Atlanta in 1925, was the first woman in the area to fly solo.

Morrison would later press local officials — and when that failed, her congressman — to build a real airport.

In 1932, an association formed to build a new air terminal. It bought 440 acres and staked out runways. The total cost of the "modern" airport was estimated at $180,000.

On Dec. 19, 1936, the airfield was dedicated. It had expanded to 598 acres, with three 3,000-foot runways, and was paid for by the county, the state and two federal agencies. It was called Morrison Field — perhaps the first such facility named for a woman.

But Grace Morrison was not there. She had been killed just months earlier, on Sept. 5, near Titusville, while driving a man identified as her half-brother to college. She was 42.

The first plane to depart, an Eastern Airlines DC-2, carried 14 passengers. That plane would later be forced down on a mountainside in southern New York state; all aboard miraculously escaped serious injury.

The first official landing at the airport carried three men, among them Grace Morrison's boss.

# One way to beat the bust: Play through

*Construction may have been stalled in the late '20s and early '30s, but resourceful folks found a way to make good use of vacant downtown land. Miniature golf on Clematis Street? Sure, right across from the Comeau building, where Via Jardin is today.* ■

GRANDPA AND CHARLOTTE, FROM IOWA TO FLORIDA
*Charlotte Chapman came to Florida in 1925, with her grandfather, Harry J. Chapman, her father, J. Leo Chapman, and her mother, Vera. Like so many others, they followed The Boom.* ■

## Chapter 7

# Growing Up Easy
## Memories of Our Town, 1925 to 1939

*by Charlotte Chapman Maurer*

We were the children of The Boom.

In my family, that momentous epoch of West Palm Beach's history was always referred to in capital letters. To the end of my father's long life he always categorized events as "during The Boom" or "after The Boom." Often he would say ruefully, "The Boom was over when we got here, but we didn't know it."

When we got here was just about when everyone else got here. Our time was 1925. Within a span of three or four years almost all the families represented in my high school graduating class of 1939 took that hopeful trip down U.S. 1 into our long narrow city.

While today's parents may worry if a child has to sit in a car for two hours, my parents in 1925 took it for granted that a 3-year-old would be a good girl on a 10-day hegira from Iowa to Florida. And I was. My grandfather was in the back seat with me, and I have heard that he kept me amused all the way down.

When Grandpa was a boy, he traveled in a covered wagon from Indiana to Iowa; he and his brother put the first plow to their father's prairie land. In 1925 our covered wagon was a Franklin touring car, open to the breezes, with isinglass curtains that didn't roll right down but had to be snapped on in case of downpours.

Our little family wasn't going into a complete unknown. A dozen or so years earlier my grandfather had responded to some Florida land promoters touring through Iowa, and he had actually gone to Palm Beach County to see the Everglades muck land they were promoting. By the time he persuaded his son, my father, that West Palm Beach was the promised land, the small city had been his winter home for some years.

### Land of dreams and opportunity

Today, when I talk about the old days with my high school classmates, I realize that most of our parents came to West Palm Beach for the same reason: to make their fortunes.

My own father was a small-town lawyer eking out a living by examining titles; he needed a better opportunity. The father of my classmate Harold

*THE KIDS OF GREYMON DRIVE*
By 1929, Charlotte had a 3-year-old sister, Fay, and friends right across the street. Bob (left) and Edward McKenna joined the Chapman girls at their favorite spot, the beach. ■

*Kenyon Riddle*

*Karl Riddle*

Merry had lost his business in Athens, Ga., paid off his debts, and migrated to West Palm Beach to start over. My friend Gloria Steed says her father was "sort of a rolling stone." When Kenyon Riddle, for whom he had worked in Ohio, asked Gloria's father to come down and join his new construction company, Mr. Steed just picked up his family and went.

Kenyon Riddle's own story is a good one.

In 1920 he was the city manager of Xenia, Ohio. At a convention, he was hired to be city manager of West Palm Beach. Being otherwise occupied at the time, he sent his twin brother Karl. "I don't think they ever knew the difference," Kenyon's daughter Nancy says now.

Karl Riddle fell in love with West Palm Beach and persuaded Kenyon to bring his family here, too. That was in 1923. The twin brothers started the Palm Beach Engineering Company, which soon built route A1A, the Boca Raton Club, Hialeah racetrack and several Palm Beach estates.

"They must have done pretty well," I said to Nancy the other day.

"I guess they did," she said, "until the crash."

## When The Boom busted

As children, were we aware that there had been a crash, that the Florida Boom was over?

Probably not, although Gloria Steed remembers a definite change in her family's life. Her father, who by then had his own construction company with an office in the Harvey Building, suddenly stopped building roads and all of his heavy equipment disappeared. They no longer had a maid and a chauffeur.

Unlike the Steeds, many newly arrived couples didn't realize The Boom was over until they had paid too much money for a scrap of land that turned worthless soon after they bought it.

But land was not worthless for building your own Florida home.

My parents found their spot in Southland Park, halfway between Belvedere and Southern Boulevard, in the block between Dixie and Olive.

With Grandpa's help, they bought two 50-foot lots at $6,000 each on adjoining streets. They hired a contractor to build a semi-Spanish-style bungalow — complete with porte-cochere, French doors and wrought-iron balconies — on one lot; the other was considered an investment. But it was too late to invest in land in West Palm Beach. The second lot was eventually lost for non-payment of taxes.

When the mid-1920s building boom on our block of Greymon Drive was finished, there were 10 houses, five facing north and five facing south. We were smack in the middle of the north side. At each end of the block were large vacant lots — we called them woods — where we children could run through our own paths, picking huckleberries in season or building small campfires and roasting potatoes in the ashes.

To the east of us, Olive Avenue — unsullied by houses and intersected by empty streets with large stone lampposts — stretched majestically down toward the Lake Worth canal. When I was around 5, my friend Bobby and I would walk down Olive almost to the canal and back again. No one worried about us.

To the far west lay one-lane Parker Avenue, and a subdivision called Hillcrest, where massive stone pillars marked the entrance to streets that stretched weedily off into nothing. Karl and Kenyon Riddle had built houses there, but they had no near neighbors. My parents used to take visitors out to see Hillcrest. "This is what happened when The Boom busted," they would say. We children stared at the pillars and wondered.

My family was luckier than many. Never having made big money in construction or real estate, my father settled quietly into the life of being a junior partner in the law firm of Kearley, Fisher, Van Metre and Chapman. I am sure that he and mother were ecstatic about their beautiful new Spanish-style home (who could have dreamed of such a house in Iowa?) and with their new baby daughter — my little sister Fay, born just before the '26 hurricane and shortly before the new house was ready. Two years later, Fay and I sat on our little wooden chairs in the solarium and watched the coconut tree outside whip back and forth in the winds of the '28 storm, while Mother and Dad and my cousin Gertrude tried to nail up the door into the back bedroom where a window had blown in.

## The beach — the center of everything

After the 1928 hurricane, West Palm Beach settled down into being a normal kind of small town with normal families trying to make a living.

The beach was, it seems, the center of everything. ("We spent most of our lives outdoors," Nancy Riddle remembers.) Depression or no Depression, the beach was free and we always had enough gas or pedal-power to get there.

My mother fell in love with the ocean and with swimming and shell collecting. My father seldom put on a bathing suit, but he loved to walk the sand with us children, poking at crab holes and turning over seaweed. Mother soon developed the custom of taking a picnic supper to the beach once each week — not sandwiches or hot dogs, but a full hot dinner cooked in a contraption called the fireless cooker.

*A FLORIDA DREAM HOME*
*With its French doors, columns and arches, the house on Greymon Drive thrilled Vera Chapman. She posed on the balcony soon after her home was finished in 1926. The interior view shows the living room and, beyond, the "solarium." This is a later photo — but the only thing that changed over the years was the addition of a television.* ∎

WATER'S EDGE
*Charlotte's mother Vera holds Fay, while Charlotte and a friend play. "Croker's beach" was a favorite spot. Richard Croker, former Tammany chieftain in New York, had a winter home on the ocean, south of Southern Boulevard.* ∎

We took our suppers to Croker's beach — and we weren't the only ones. Some evenings there would be a row of picnicking families, their campfires flickering, as far as we could see in either direction. We would go over as soon as Dad got home from the office, spread out the blankets and then walk for a while until we were good and hungry. Then Mother would take the two aluminum pots out of the fireless cooker and dish up our supper. We'd sit and watch our beloved ocean, and sometimes a spectacular reflected sunset, until it was almost dark, and we'd go home feeling happy.

Some time during those years Mother decided that she and my sister and I should learn to swim properly, and she bought a booklet by the great swimmer Johnny Weismuller on how to do the Australian crawl. Our next-door neighbor, Richard Middleton, was the manager of the Bath and Tennis Club in Palm Beach. During the summer, while the members were at other playgrounds, he let us use the Bath and Tennis Club pool. Mother and Fay and I, alone in that magnificent swimming space, followed the pictured instructions and taught ourselves to do the crawl.

My joy was climbing to the platform that led to the high board and, holding my nose, jumping 14 feet into the deep end. Many years later, driving around that curve in the road that borders the Bath and Tennis Club wall, I would look over at the high board. "I used to jump off that when I was a kid," I'd tell my own kids.

## Can a peasant admire a king? Absolutely

Much as we Boom children like to suppress the fact that our fathers *didn't* make their fortunes by moving to Florida, much as we might like to forget that our families were often in touch-and-go, sometimes desperate, situations, we finally have to admit it. Most of us were poor. It wasn't a word that we used much — or if we did, it was always about other people — but looking back, we can remember.

I remember my father sitting alone in the office he had rented after he lost his junior partnership with Kearley and Fisher. Dad's secretary, in the front room, was also alone. She was filing her fingernails, and Dad was reading a magazine.

I remember my grandfather, for no reason at all, putting an envelope under Mother's plate at breakfast one morning. (That was the way we always gave presents, by putting them under the overturned plate.) Mother opened it and started crying. The note inside said that from now on Grandpa was going to give her $50 a month to pay for his room and board.

I remember when I was applying for a scholarship to Rollins College in 1939, that my father had to fill out financial statements. I wasn't supposed to see them, but somehow I did. To my horror, I discovered that Dad's income for each of the previous two years had been less than $2,000.

I remember men coming to the back door, knocking, and asking humbly for food. I remember Mother hurrying to heap up plates, and the men quietly eating at the back porch table.

I remember that our allowance for meat for an evening meal for five people was 35 cents. Thirty-five cents would buy a pound of round steak — ground twice — a can of salmon, a package of dried beef or a can of corned beef hash.

I remember that we always ate well. So we couldn't have been poor. We weren't hungry, we were beautifully housed, my sister and I got new school dresses every year, and we had a Franklin car — a square black one that had replaced the old touring car.

The car was our chariot, our entree to other worlds — especially Palm Beach. Can a peasant look at a king? Absolutely.

During the season we would park on Worth Avenue and walk up one side and down the other, commenting on the merchandise in every window, choosing what we would buy if we happened to belong on Worth Avenue. Sometimes we would simply park the car on another street and walk for a while studying the houses. Sometimes we made an excursion to the polo games, which were held on a field in Delray.

So we knew how the rich lived, and we accepted them as part of our lives — although they didn't, I presume, accept us. I can't remember any

DO YOU REMEMBER . . . ?

*"When so many students moved to Florida from the Midwest with their midwestern accents. They read 'perms' in school, and 'changed the erl in their caws.' But all the 'dis, dats, the youse and the you'alls' blended together, and we became friends . . .*

*"All the kids said 'yes, sir,' and 'no, ma'am,' they kept their hair combed and polished their shoes. This was without doubt the squarest and corniest generation that ever clawed its way through life."*

■ *Palm Beach High reunion book for the classes of 1938 to 1942*

resentment, any revolution-inciting thoughts about why they had so much and we so little. If there were revolutionaries in West Palm Beach, they didn't move in our circle.

## First Presbyterian: Our congregation of friends

My parents' circle revolved almost entirely around the First Presbyterian Church. In 1925, the congregation met in a tiny white frame building on Iris Street west of Dixie.

There, Mother and Dad found all the friends they ever needed. All the young couples — the Carmichaels, the Allens, the Hitts, the Campbells, the Frasers, the Corwins, the Chapmans, the Geislers, the Vivians, the Schroeders — most of them newly arrived, coalesced into a congenial group that remained friends as long as they lived. Mother immediately became the soprano soloist in the choir, and Dad contributed his rich bass undertone to the men's section.

The ladies had their organization, called The Wheel, that met every week at someone's house to do good works, chat, laugh, and eat. When it was Nell Vivian's turn to host the meeting, the ladies made a point of posing for a picture around the swimming pool; Homer Vivian was caretaker of a Palm Beach estate.

**POSING BY THE POOL**

*Charlotte's mother and her friends got a taste of the Palm Beach life when their church group, The Wheel, met at Nell Vivian's house. Mr. Vivian was caretaker of a Palm Beach estate.* ◼

## Dance and piano: Lots of culture for 50 cents

During those years when money was scarce, Mother and Dad's one form of entertainment was their weekly vocal lessons. These cost, I believe, one dollar each, or perhaps a dollar for both. Nor did they neglect the cultural education of us girls. They bought a piano, and for a year or two I faithfully practiced, until the insistent whispers from outside the French doors, "Charlotte! When can you come out and play?" made me persuade Mother to let me quit. Probably she was glad to save the 50 cents.

But there was enough money for dancing lessons. For years my sister and I and our friends went to a woman's house for dancing school. Even little boys learned to dance, and when we had struggled together though the waltz and the foxtrot, we advanced to the latest Fred Astaire creations like the Continental.

And there was enough money for the movies. Every Saturday morning, our parents gave us 15 cents a week allowance and sent us downtown to the Stanley Theater, on Clematis in the block west of Dixie, where they showed the serials we loved. Just before 1 o'clock on Saturday afternoon, dozens of kids from all over town would be milling around outside until someone opened the ticket window and took our dimes. Inside, it was a great big noisy party. We whooped and hollered and screamed as each serial reached its "to be continued next week" climax.

## School days: Oleanders for my teacher

Besides going to the beach, the pool and the movies, we did go to school. I started Southboro School, on Nottingham west of Dixie, in the fall of 1928. It became my second home for six years, yet I can't remember ever being taken there in a car. We walked the mile-and-a-half to school — one of the most pleasant parts of our day. In spring, when the oleanders were blooming, a friend and I would each take a large grocery sack and pick oleanders for the teacher all the way to Southboro. I often wonder how she managed to deal with those fragrant masses of flowers.

Soon all of us from Southboro were joined by our compatriots from Palmetto School, in the far south part of town, at Conniston Road Junior High. Conniston Road School was, then, a small white frame building with a porch and steps in front, a central open space that served as auditorium and lunch room, and three classrooms on each side. Somewhere there was room for a kitchen, where the cafeteria ladies prepared our delicious (yes!) 15-cent lunches. We always hoped for apple cake with whipped cream for dessert.

*BALLET DAYS*
*All the neighborhood kids learned to dance — even Charlotte.* ∎

*FRIENDS IN JUNIOR HIGH, FRIENDS FOREVER*
*Charlotte's friends from Conniston: Hazel Hime, Gloria Steed, Marie Van Son and Helen Woodward, in the driveway on Greymon Drive.* ∎

SHE MADE
IT HERSELF
*All grown up:
Charlotte around
1937, showing off a
dress she made in high-
school Home Ec.* ∎

One of the students who came up from Palmetto was Gloria Steed, who became my close friend and remains so. Shortly before we graduated from Conniston, she and I — plus Helen, Hazel and Marie — decided we would each have a luncheon party for the others. Our mothers cooperated enthusiastically, spreading the table with the best cloth and letting us use their prettiest dishes and silver.

## "Gimme a hamburger C.K. please."

At last came the crown of our young lives — Palm Beach High School. In September 1936 we arrived at the big school on the hill — some of us from Conniston, some from Central Junior High, which was just next door, some from Northboro, and a few of us came from Palm Beach.

On Fridays — game days during football season — the whole school cheered at the pep rallies ("Palm Beach will shine tonight!") and went to the game. I joined the girls' drill team so I could get in free. Our team was always good, but, being a relatively small school, we very seldom beat Miami Edison.

It wasn't so with baseball. In our junior year Palm Beach High took the state championship, and all of us girls became baseball fans. Someone arranged a post-season series with the champions of Georgia, which our team won, and then they played the champions of North and South Carolina with the same happy result.

That summer we spent a lot of time in the old wooden grandstand, admiring Van Kinnamon on the mound or at first base, instead of going to the beach. That was the summer I made all my own clothes (Home Ec was required in our sophomore year), and decided that I would wear nothing but white and black.

Our Boom generation class was the largest yet — 255 of us graduated — and we enjoyed being with each other. At lunchtime, rather than eat in the cafeteria, we would take our 30 cents across the street to the Campus Shop and buy a half-pint of milk and a Ration bar — chocolate-covered graham crackers. Then we'd sit on the concrete wall around the school yard while we ate and kibitzed.

If we didn't buy a second Ration bar, there'd be a dime left for a limeade at Walgreens after school. We'd sit at the Walgreens counter and sip the limeade, then maybe wander through Woolworth's, maybe visit my father in his new office in the Comeau Building, before catching the southbound bus on Dixie. Alas, we thought it perfectly natural that people whose faces were darker than ours sat in the back.

Evenings would often find us at The Hut, that famous drive-in at the bend in Flagler Drive near Trinity Place. I've often bragged in later years

CAMPUS SHOP: A HANGOUT FOR 50 YEARS

*This photo of the Campus Shop ran in the 1954 Palm Beach High yearbook, but the action was the same in Charlotte's Class of '39 as it was in '54. The caption says: "Munchin' their luncheon." The Campus Shop closed in the late '60s because of racial unrest. It reopened briefly in 1986, but closed again.* ■

that Florida was ahead of the rest of the world. We had supermarkets in the '20s and drive-ins in the '30s. The Hut must surely have been one of the first places to serve a hamburger with everything — "clean kitchen," we called it, or C.K. "Gimme a hamburger C.K. please." The Hut's parking lot would be filled with cars that were filled with our friends, and the music would be blaring from the jukebox inside.

## The best part about being in the Comrad Club

There was a sophisticated crowd at school, to which I did not belong. They were the boys and girls in the Greek-letter fraternities and sororities. Next down on the social scale were clubs, which operated exactly the same way as fraternities: college-style rushing, then pledging, then initiation.

During my junior year I was pleased to be rushed and asked to pledge by the Comrad Club (I had been ignored as a sophomore). I remember that during a certain week we pledges were instructed to wear as much makeup as we could possibly put on. My parents were dubious and my teachers must have been shocked, but it was the first time I got any attention. People kept coming up to me and saying, "Charlotte! I didn't know you had such long eyelashes!"

The best part about being a member of a club or sorority was what happened to celebrate graduation. Each group would take a house in Palm Beach for the following week. Our rental at 135 Worth Ave. cost $50, as I remember it. A cook was hired and, according to *The Post-Times*, Mrs. Brooke Rhodes was our chaperone. We girls slept in cots on an upstairs sleeping porch where we got the ocean breeze. *The Post-Times* reported that we had "swimming parties and midnight feasts with open houses for parents and friends," but mostly I remember us sitting on the beds, eating chocolates and reading romantic magazines that were supposed to be shocking.

## Goodbye to friends — and childhood

And then high school was over.

Was graduation night, with the full moon rising over the back of the band shell in the West Palm Beach City Park, the end of our lives together? For the children of The Boom, it certainly foreshadowed the end.

The year was 1939, remember. On a Sunday in early September, the day before I was to leave for Rollins College, the Nazis invaded Poland. I told my father there was no point in my going to college now since there was obviously going to be another world war. "You *are* going to college," was his only response.

But many of my classmates did not have even my family's limited resources. Most of them couldn't dream of further education. Some enrolled at Palm Beach Junior College, which was just like continuing high school since the college was in one small building across from Palm Beach High. Some found jobs.

It was two years before the United States was officially in the good war, but it was less time than that before men began to be drafted. Many of the boys in my class (we called them boys in those days), headed off to serve — and the children of The Boom began to scatter.

We had grown up in an easy time in an easy place.

Although our fathers hadn't made their fortunes, they had brought us to the promised land, and we were at home there.

THE WALKS WE'LL ALWAYS REMEMBER
*Gloria Steed and Charlotte Chapman on Palm Beach, 1939.* ■

## FEAR, INTRIGUE AND ROMANCE

*In West Palm Beach, World War II was close enough to see. "We couldn't go up on the oceanfront after dark," remembers Bobby Riggs, who grew up in West Palm Beach. "I was sitting at The Hut one night and the whole sky lit up. The Germans had sunk a tanker off Palm Beach." Germans sank 24 ships off Florida's coast. One of them, the Cities Service Empire, is shown below in a photograph taken from the U.S.S. Biddle. Because news was delayed (The Palm Beach Post reported the incidents a few days later), rumors and fear abounded. Rationing was tough, too, recalls Riggs, who graduated from Palm Beach High in 1943. But leaving for war was tougher. On graduation night, he and some friends went out to the Palm Beach Pier one last time and started to cry. Their carefree boyhood was over; in days, they'd be overseas. For those who stayed home, memories are bittersweet. Canteens (such as this one in Palm Beach, below) and U.S.O. clubs entertained the thousands of GIs stationed here. The intensity of war made even the simplest pleasures grand.* ∎

THE PALM BEACH POST

WEST PALM BEACH, FLORIDA, WEDNESDAY MORNING, FEBRUARY 25, 1942

orpedoings Off Coast Announ

Survivors Of Empire
And Republic Landed
Nearby, Navy Reveals

Two Vessels Believed To

WAR RATION BOOK No. 305d

*Chapter 8*

# The War Years

## 1941-1945

West Palm Beach's mothers sent their sons to the "good war" and dutifully placed blue stars in their windows. As World War II took its toll, gold stars replaced some of the blue ones — two from Pearl Harbor, then more and more, bad news from strange places a world away.

But in South Florida the war was not all overseas. Here, it was close enough for people to feel the heat and see the flames of the ships being picked off night after night by the stealthy sharks that were the *Unterseeboots* of the Third Reich.

Only those who have lived in war zones can comprehend the fear with which South Floridians went to bed each night, wondering if a shell would crash down on them as they slept.

And the military came. Florida, a strategic asset for its geography and climate, became an armed camp. Its hotels turned into barracks. Hospitals, bases and airfields sprang up. Military installations statewide increased from eight in 1940 to 172 in 1943. After the war, many bases were transformed to public use.

Soldiers heading home from war got heroes' welcomes as their trains passed through West Palm Beach. Those who had been stationed in South Florida went home with stories of the paradise they had left, and many later returned to stay.

That migration changed Florida's population from about 2 million in 1940 to nearly 3 million a decade later. Another Florida boom was on the way.

*"SO MUCH IN LOVE"*
*Amid the rationing and the worries, love blossomed. "This photo was taken in downtown West Palm Beach," says Lucy Seader. "My sailor man came home on leave, and we got married Feb. 21, 1943 . . . and so much in love."* ■

# Key events, 1941-1945

*CLEMATIS STREET, 1941*
*The Pioneer store — which sold furni-*
*ture and carpet then and now sells*
*linens — remains on Clematis Street*
*today.* ■

*COAST GUARD RESERVE*
*Lt. Gleason Stambaugh retrieves bodies*
*as the Gulf Bell burns. (It had collided*
*with the Gulfland during a blackout.)* ■

**Feb. 27, 1941:**
Morrison Field officially
becomes an Army post,
although civilian air traffic
continues.

**Dec. 7, 1941:**
Morrison Field Army Air
Force Command activated.
Effort to reactivate Palm
Beach County Fair, dor-
mant during Depression,
scuttled by beginning of
war.

**1942-1945:** Military
bases and personnel fill
Florida. German U-boats
sink 16 ships between Cape
Canaveral and Boca Raton
from February to May
1942. Local Coast Guard
Reserve, headed by

Gleason Stambaugh, aids
in saving crew members
from burning ships.

**Jan. 11, 1942:** Practice
blackout throws Palm
Beaches into darkness.

**Jan. 19, 1942:** Air
Transport Command
begins operation, increases
the airport to 2,270 acres.
Runways, taxiway lights, a
control tower, aprons,
ramps, roadways and water
and sewer systems are built
by government.

**Dec. 11, 1942:** The
Breakers hotel comman-
deered by Army, becomes
Ream General Hospital.

# The war off our shore

In the first half-year of World War II, the Germans sank 397 ships off the American coast in the Atlantic Ocean and Gulf of Mexico and killed some 5,000 people — about twice as many as died in Hawaii on Dec. 7, 1941.

Off Florida alone, Germans sank 24 ships — 16 of them from Cape Canaveral to Boca Raton — between February and May 1942. Subs sometimes sank ships hours apart. The deadliest stretch came in May, when 10 ships sank in 10 days, seven of them between Fort Pierce and Boca Raton.

The Florida attacks killed hundreds of men and sent millions of dollars in cargo and oil to the bottom. Men aboard Coast Guard and Navy ships and volunteers rescued about 500 seamen, many badly burned, and saved some of the cargo.

About one of every 12 ships sunk worldwide in 1942 went down in Florida waters, reports said.

ON FIRE, 1942
*A tanker, believed to be the Halsey, burns off Jupiter Island.* ■

# We're in the Army now

Morrison Field was home base to 3,000 personnel during the war. About 45,000 fliers trained at or left from the field, and about 6,000 planes passed through in the eight months before D-Day. The base also maintained many giant C-54 cargo planes that "flew the Hump" — the dangerous air route over the Himalayas — to supply Chinese fighting the Japanese invasion.

Camp Murphy — now Jonathan Dickinson State Park — in southern Martin County was the Army's Southern Signal Corps School. It trained 5,000 to 10,000 men.

The Boca Raton Army Air Field was set up as an Army Air Corps training site and radar training base. The property was later split; half became a municipal airport and the other half Florida Atlantic University. Former runways are now student parking lots.

Oceanfront hotels were commandeered by the military. The Breakers in Palm Beach became Ream General Hospital. The Biltmore was lent to the U.S. Coast Guard.

Prisoner-of-war camps were set up in the sugar-growing areas around Lake Okeechobee, and Germans were put to work in the fields. After the war, the camps were torn down, replaced by more rows of sugar cane.

MORRISON FIELD
*Taken over by the Army in 1941 and for the duration of the war, it was the forerunner of Palm Beach International Airport.* ■

# The homefront:
## Watches and rumors

WAR ENTRANCE
*Grace Frost England in front of Wert's restaurant in Palm Beach, now Charley's Crab. (Their slogan: "Everyone goes from bad to Wert's.") The entrance was moved from the oceanfront to the side to prevent light from shining out at sea. It remains on the side today.* ■

Everything changed when the war came to West Palm Beach.

Beachfront hotels, homes and restaurants dimmed their lights so German subs couldn't spot tankers off shore.

Street lights were hooded to cast only a small circle of light directly down. Patrol dogs ran people off the beaches at night.

The Coast Guard set up observation towers every 3 miles, at places like the Lake Worth casino.

Anyone crossing the bridges to Palm Beach encountered an armed sentry who shined his flashlight, demanded identification and sometimes searched cars. To get across, residents had to be fingerprinted and photographed for an I.D. card.

Jumpy authorities rounded up virtually anyone with a German-sounding accent or Asian features. By late February 1942, news reports showed FBI agents made 55 raids in the West Palm Beach and Fort Lauderdale areas, arresting 29 suspected enemy aliens and confiscating guns and cameras.

On "the hill" — the complex that housed Palm Beach High School, junior high and elementary — stories of sinkings, attacks and Germans coming ashore flew through classrooms. Teachers would hush students, saying, "If you didn't see it, don't talk about it. The enemy might be listening."

Many rumors emerged in the war years and have since been discounted. Among them:

■ U-boat crews surrendered in Jupiter or Palm Beach or were held at the downtown West Palm Beach Burdines.

■ The George Washington Hotel's roof lights blinked code to offshore U-boats.

■ Military planes bombed a U-boat found in an inlet behind a Palm Beach woman's estate.

■ Searches found Holsum Bread wrappers and Florida Theater movie tickets on U-boat crews.

■ German sailors snuck ashore and had drinks at Palm Beach's TaBoo nightclub.

## DOING THEIR PART

The Breakers became Ream General Hospital during the war. One of the glamorous ballrooms was transformed for a holiday prayer vigil (above). The Junior Women's Club rallied for the GIs, handing out watermelons and plenty of good cheer (right). ■

# What I remember . . .

Kay Hutchins, 1942

"**I** was in my early 20s when 'the boys' arrived to activate the new Army Air Corps base at Morrison Field in 1941. When 3,000 young men hit town, it was a bonanza beyond compare for single girls! As a volunteer at the Servicemen's Center in downtown West Palm Beach, I met many GIs."

— *Kay Hutchins, West Palm Beach*

"**E**very Saturday from 10 a.m. to noon during 1942 and 1943, my dear friend Louise (now in Fort Pierce) and I were airplane spotters in the Aircraft Warning Service, U.S. Army.

"The spotter post was a room on the roof of the Harvey Building in downtown West Palm Beach. We were cautioned not to report bobbing coconuts (there were lots then) or pelicans (lots of them, too) in our excitement.

"The most frightening, exciting watch we had was the morning we turned our binoculars to the west and in amazement saw dusty pink planes circling and landing at Morrison Field! We grabbed the phone! We were informed that the African campaign had begun, and these planes were camouflaged for desert terrain.

"A footnote to this: We lived on Greymon Drive, in the takeoff corridor, and night after night we lay in bed, or were awakened in the wee hours, and counted the steady columns of planes departing. The record was 45."

— *Kathleen R. Pacetti, West Palm Beach*

"**O**n Saturday nights, Clematis Street was jammed with soldiers going in and out of the stores, sipping sodas at Walgreens, guzzling a beer at the Toro Lounge. Of course, we walked everywhere because very few young people or GIs had cars.

"Cy's Men's Store did a big business dressing the survivors of some of those oil tankers that were blown out of the water. At the local night spots, they were usually celebrating the survivors — on the house, of course.

"Since we could not use car lights (or any outside lights) in Palm Beach because of blackout orders, fender benders were common. We solved that problem by riding the ferry from the G.W. Hotel (the George Washington, now the Helen Wilkes Hotel) over to the Biltmore Hotel. The captain only had one arm, which sometimes interfered with his navigation. Five cents a ride, with entertainment thrown in."

— *Dora Digby, Palm Beach*

"**W**e lived out the war years, partly in total blackness as the German subs lay off the coastline ready to pick off ships. While in total blackout, we witnessed several encounters offshore — flares, rockets, gunfire. Since security was tight, we never knew exactly what we were seeing.

"By daylight, we watched an incredible sight as hundreds of ships moved across the horizon heading south.

"Mother was a member of the Motor Corps and learned to take apart an engine. She also distributed meat, butter and sugar stamps to long lines of locals — we were all rationed."

— *Joy S. Kissam, North Palm Beach*

*Joy Kissam and her future husband, Hunter, in Palm Beach, 1942.*

AT LAST
IT WAS OVER
*Frances M.*
*Stambaugh, Miss*
*West Palm Beach of*
*1945, shows soldiers*
*the good news, as*
*reported by* The Palm
Beach Times. ■

"**I** was on the night shift on what was the old second floor at Good Samaritan Hospital. I went into the utility room to warm a pitcher of water on a two-burner gas stove. Suddenly, I heard a boom, and my little pitcher bounced about an inch off the stove! No one knew what shook everything so much. Two hours later, we found out in a horrible fashion: They started bringing in sailors from a ship that had been torpedoed off the shore by U-boats. These men were all European, spoke no English and were so burned and swollen, we could not tell what they looked like."

— *Carolyn B.*
*Darr, Jupiter*

*Carolyn B. Darr, 1942*

"**W**e had a manual telephone switchboard in Lake Worth — the kind where the operator said, 'Number please. Thank you.' About 4 o'clock one morning in 1942 a call came in from Harold Vanderbilt, who lived on the ocean in Manalapan. He said, 'Operator, there's a ship on fire.' Mr. Vanderbilt called his friends in Palm Beach, and they brought their big coffee urns and blankets for the boys, who had to swim through burning oil to get to shore at Boynton Inlet."

— *Florence B. Schnopp, Lake Worth*

"**I** was a *Palm Beach Times* paper boy, and I sold 150 'Extras' on the day the war was over in Europe. I went all through the neighborhood, yelling and shouting 'Extra' — and people were rushing to their windows."

— *Moses B. Stubbs Jr., West Palm Beach*

"**O**ur mayor called me and asked me to rush down to the West Palm Beach train station and tell a train full of servicemen coming from Miami that the war was over and we had won! It was one of the most exciting moments of my life to see the joy on the faces of these men."

— *Frances M. Stambaugh, West Palm Beach*

HEART OF WEST PALM BEACH, 1952
*Phillips Point is at the bottom of the photograph. The Pennsylvania Hotel, the Hotel Salt Air and the George Washington (formerly the El Verano Hotel) can be seen at the curve of the waterfront to the north. Flagler Drive was still two lanes in the '50s.* ■

## Chapter 9

# Prime Time
## 1945-1963

Ask a West Palm Beach native to describe the post-war years, and you'll hear the same words over and over: Fun, innocence, stability. And *happiness*.

"There was a richness to it all," remembers Monte Markham, the television actor who was president of Palm Beach High's Class of 1953. "I don't think there is anything like it now short of living in a small town in Iowa. There was no violence, no drugs. Something as weird as the *a capella* choir — the men's glee club — was a big thing to get into. People just laughed and smiled and joked.

"It was *Happy Days*."

South Florida's confidence was back.

Buoyed by military dollars during World War II and an influx of veterans moving south, West Palm Beach was ready to enter a new era of progress.

The city's total property value rose from a rock-bottom $18 million in 1935 to $72 million in 1949 and continued to surge year by year until it was $147.5 million by 1962 — an eight-fold increase in less than 30 years.

The metropolitan area was the fourth fastest growing place in the country between 1950 and 1960. Development spread west past Military Trail and south to Lake Clarke Shores.

Ads in *The Palm Beach Post* touted "new prestige neighborhoods" of concrete block homes in "suburban community villages." What could be finer than a three-bedroom, swimming pool home with central air — for just $14,950?

And then, to top it all off, a set of rabbit ears and a television.

The first TV station — WIRK, Channel 21 — came to town in 1953, and channels 5 and 12 followed a couple years later. Before long, everyone was getting their news from Bill Gordon on WPTV, and Tony Glenn's *Let's Dance* show tapped into the new rock 'n' roll craze.

But people in West Palm Beach didn't stick glued to their sets — not yet. With the pier, The Hut and the baseball diamond, they still spent most of their happy days out in the sun.

*Advertisements from* The Palm Beach Post, *the 1950s.* ■

# Key events: 1945-1963

**1947:** Mangonia Park, Glen Ridge incorporated.

**Sept. 17, 1947:** Hurricane brings storm surges of 22 feet around Lake Okeechobee; dike holds.

**Oct. 12, 1947:** Hurricane causes worst flooding on record. Central and Southern Florida Flood Control District formed; becomes South Florida Water Management District.

**Dec. 17, 1947:** Terminal opens at Palm Beach International Airport, formerly Morrison Field.

*New airport terminal, 1947.*

**May 10, 1948:** New City Hall opens on Second Street, across from county courthouse.

**June 2, 1949:** Highland Beach incorporated.

**Aug. 26, 1949:** Hurricane strikes Palm Beach County coast and Glades, causing minor damage.

**1950:** Population: Florida: 2,771,305, Palm Beach County 114,688, West Palm Beach 43,162.

**May 3, 1950:** Haverhill incorporated.

**Fall, 1950:** Industrial High School for blacks absorbed by Roosevelt High.

**Sept. 15, 1950:** Southern Boulevard bridge to Palm Beach opens.

**1951:** Cloud Lake and Palm Beach Shores incorporated.

**Sept. 16, 1951:** During Korean War, portion of airport reactivated as Palm Beach Air Base.

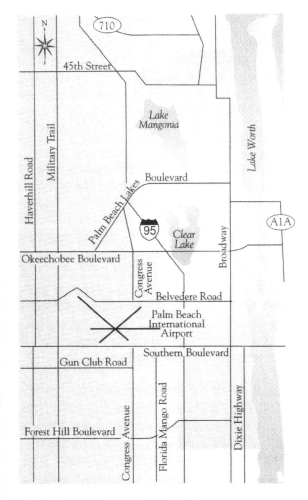

*City limits in 1948 (in yellow), charted on a 1994 base map.*

**June 17, 1953:** Juno Beach incorporated.

**Sept. 13, 1953:** WIRK-TV, Channel 21, area's first television station, signs on.

**Aug. 22, 1954:** WJNO-TV, Channel 5, (NBC) signs on. Becomes WPTV in 1956.

**Jan. 1, 1955:** WEAT-TV (later WPEC), Channel 12 (ABC), signs on.

**May-July 1955:** South Palm Beach and Hypoluxo incorporated.

**June 15, 1955:** Circuit Judge C.E. Chillingworth and wife murdered at sea.

**Nov. 30, 1955:** City buys water plant from Flagler estate, ending a monopoly on water and sewer dating back to incorporation.

**1956:** North Palm Beach incorporated.

**Jan. 25, 1957:** Sunshine State Parkway, now Florida's Turnpike, opens.

**May-July 1957:** Village of Golf, Tequesta, Palm Springs, Lake Clarke Shores incorporated.

**Sept. 9, 1957:** City sells about 5,500 acres to Westward Development Associates, which will develop sprawling Palm Beach Lakes area.

**January 1958:** Palm Beach County Fair moves to current location west of Florida's Turnpike on Southern Boulevard.

**May 27, 1958:** Pratt & Whitney opens plant on 7,000-acre campus in northwest Palm Beach County to develop and test jet and rocket engines.

**Aug. 13, 1958:** Beeline Highway opens.

**Sept. 2, 1958:** Forest Hill, the city's second public high school for whites, opens.

**September 1958:** Roosevelt Junior College for blacks opens.

**1959:** Palm Beach Gardens, Atlantis, Jupiter Inlet Colony and Royal Palm Beach incorporated.

**May 16, 1959:** New Royal Park Bridge (middle bridge) to Palm Beach opens.

**Nov. 12, 1959:** Palm Coast Plaza opens as city's first shopping mall.

**1960:** Population: Florida: 4,951,560; Palm Beach County 228,106, West Palm Beach 56,208.

**May 24, 1961:** RCA opens $4 million plant in Palm Beach Gardens.

**April 1962:** WTVX-TV, Channel 34 in Fort Pierce, signs on.

*Library in 1962.*

**April 30, 1962:** Present library opens.

**March 9, 1963:** West Palm Beach Municipal Stadium opens.

**June 19, 1963:** Briny Breezes incorporated.

*President Kennedy at St. Ann Church, Nov. 17.*

**Nov. 16-17, 1963:** President John F. Kennedy spends last weekend of his life in Palm Beach.

# Happy days: Having fun and hanging out

## PALM BEACH PIER

In the '40s, Worth Avenue extended right out over the water, thanks to the Palm Beach Pier. On the pier was a coffee shop, a bait and tackle shop and a place where you could rent rods and reels. "The beach was wide, particularly in front of Gus' Baths, which later became the Lido Pools (Gus' Baths was just south of the pier, across the street)," remembers Bobby Riggs. The pier was condemned in 1966 after a storm damaged it, and it was later torn down. ■

In post-war West Palm Beach, the mood was up, the teens were "hep" and the relaxation was as wonderful as the weather.

## TEEN TOWN: JUST A LITTLE TOO SQUARE

The West Palm Beach Jaycees considered it "the answer to the challenge of youth" — Teen Town, a youth center that opened in a portion of Howard Park in 1949. The kids helped build it and it had its own government. It also had "everything a kid could want: A soda fountain, table tennis, a dance floor," remembers Bobby Riggs, who was 24 when it opened. "But nobody came. It was too neat, too organized — just too square for them." ■

## LET'S GO TO THE HUT

*The Hut — West Palm's hangout to beat all hangouts — was so all-American that Saturday Evening Post featured it (and this photo) in its June 22, 1946, issue. "Those were the days of convertibles and cruisin' around," remembers Dick Hall, 71, whose father Harold opened The Hut in 1930 between Flagler Drive and Holy Trinity Episcopal Church. Dick worked "behind the counter and hopped curb" from 1930 to 1937, when his dad sold The Hut to Mel Williams. When Williams joined the Navy in World War II, Harold Hall continued to run The Hut. "We had curb girls in those days — Dixie Flanagan was one of the favorites," says Dick Hall, who remembers the "hamburgs and barbecue" most fondly. Bobby Riggs, who graduated in Palm Beach High's Class of 1943, remembers the Coney Island Cheesits — hot dogs split open and filled with cheese. "For years, I dreamed about having enough money to get one." The average check in the '40s was 60 cents. After the war, the Hall family opened Hall Hardware on Dixie Highway. In later years, The Hut went through a succession of owners, finally closing permanently to make way for the Phillips Point office tower in the early '80s.* ∎

## COTTON CLUB SOUTH

"Have you ever heard of the Cotton Club in Harlem?" Nat Lane of West Palm Beach said in 1990. "That's how this place used to be here. This was our showplace." From the '30s through the early '60s, the Sunset Cocktail Lounge in West Palm Beach's Northwest neighborhood attracted musical greats such as Louis Armstrong, Ella Fitzgerald, Count Basie and Duke Ellington. The house band, the Sunset Royal Entertainers, was famous itself, performing at the Apollo Theater in New York and elsewhere. "We'd have tables decorated with flowers up on the balcony. Everybody would bring covered dishes, and eat, drink and be merry," owner Thelma Starks recalls. "It was very glamorous." And popular — sometimes nearly 2,000 people would fill the club (such as the night shown above). Integration in the mid-'60s changed things, as other clubs opened to blacks. Today (left), the Sunset struggles to stay alive, "but it's just not the same," Starks says. ■

## HEY, KIDS! REMEMBER THE PALMS AND FLORIDA THEATERS?

*And remember the fun shows? For six RC bottle caps, kids could get into the fun show at the Florida and Palms theaters downtown and the Lake Theatre in Lake Worth for free. Youngsters enjoyed a cartoon, a serial, a filmed horse race on which they could "wager" for treats, and usually a really cool monster movie. At right, the Summer Fun Show lets out at the Florida Theatre, which opened Dec. 23, 1949, on the site of the old Palms Hotel. The Kettler Theatre across the street had been renovated and renamed the Palms Theatre. This photo from 1962 (above) shows a gathering of Palm Beach Post and Times newsboys. Three years later, the Palms was leveled. In 1981, the Florida showed its last movie and became a stage theater. That closed in 1991, and a nightclub is scheduled to move in in 1994.* ■

## GIANT BANYAN TREE AND ALFAR CREAMERY

*How big was that tree on Lakeview Avenue (where Esperanté is now)? So big it
was a tourist attraction — 60 feet around the trunk, with limbs that spanned
200 feet. And Alfar Creamery, advertised on top of the soda shop, was a special
spot, too. The dairy, along the railroad tracks west of Dixie between Flamingo
Drive and Claremore Drive, was owned by native Swede Alf R. (hence the*

name Alfar) Nielson. It opened in 1931, and soon, its "Dixie Cups" were famous. They featured pictures of the latest movie stars under the lids. At that time, skim milk was considered a waste, so Nielson added chocolate to it and gave it away as free chocolate milk. The creamery was eventually sold to T.G. Lee and then to McArthur Dairy, which operates a plant on the site today. ▪

## CAREFREE THEATRE
## AND FLAMINGO PARK

A 1951 ad called the Carefree Center the "Playhouse of the Palm Beaches." It opened in 1939 as the Carefree Bowlaway (right) in the heart of the Flamingo Park business district on Dixie and Flamingo. The Carefree Theatre featured the premiere of Portrait of Jennie in 1948 (left). Flamingo Park was the first business district in West Palm Beach south of Okeechobee Road. An important figure in the area for years was Zed "Doc" Myers, who owned the Southland Pharmacy (below) across the street from the Carefree. His lunch counter was legendary — especially if you wanted to gossip about the neighbors in adjacent Flamingo Park and El Cid. ■

With more than 4,000 works, the Norton Gallery of Art is one of the Southeast's most prestigious museums. Ralph Norton, head of giant Acme Steel, founded the gallery and art school in 1941 in Pioneer Park on Olive Avenue south of downtown. He donated the waterfront land east of the gallery to the city for use as a park. Paul Manship's statue of Diana (left) was a popular subject for the art school's classes. The school closed in 1986, but the gallery is expanding — and approximately 325,000 people visit it each year. ■

## JOHNNY'S PLAYLAND

This unusual building — the oldest in the city — was originally the Dade County State Bank, founded in 1893 in Palm Beach. It was moved to Clematis Street and later became the Sheen Real Estate Office (see Page 78). But by the '40s, the building had been moved to Myrtle Street (adjacent to City Park), and it had a funnier calling. Johnny's Playland was a hit with kids, who bought their X-ray glasses, fake doggie doo and other novelties from Johnny Eggert, who also owned The Campus Shop. In 1976, Johnny's widow, Crystal, gave the building to the city. Today, it houses the Palm Beach High museum. ■

## DREHER PARK ZOO: BEGUN WITH $18 AND LOTS OF LOVE

*Paul Albert Dreher, the city's first director of parks, was instrumental in filling marshes and building Currie, Phipps and Howard parks. But he's best-remembered for his zoo. In 1951, the city paid the state $100 for the 108-acre Bacon Park, at what is now Southern Boulevard and Interstate 95. With almost no city money, Dreher — the "Johnny Appleseed of West Palm Beach," right — stocked the park with trees, plants and shrubs. Then he built a tiny red barn and spent $18 to stock it with a goat, two chickens, two ducks and a goose. (Above, Jeffrey Gomersall and Todd Kouns watch zoo keeper John McElroy feed "Bambi," who arrived in 1963.) The park was named for Dreher in 1957. The South Florida Science Museum opened next door in 1961, and the planetarium was added in 1965. Dreher died at 90 on March 17, 1993. By then, the zoo bearing his name housed more than 500 animals.* ■

## KENNEL CLUB AND JAI ALAI

*The Palm Beach Kennel Club opened on Feb. 17, 1932, during the depths of the Depression, in swamp and sand north of what is now Palm Beach International Airport. It underwent three ownership changes before Art Rooney, owner of the Pittsburgh Steelers, bought it in 1970. His family still owns it. Palm Beach Jai Alai opened in 1956 on 45th Street. On Christmas Day 1978, a fire destroyed the fronton. Police called it arson, but no one was ever charged, and the fronton reopened two years later. Players staged a walkout in 1988, the same year the state instituted the Florida Lottery. By the time the fronton reopened in 1991, it had lost its customer base. The kennel club bought the property, and the players performed for the last time on Nov. 27, 1993, although the new owners said they planned to continue jai alai there on a smaller scale. Below, a kennel club ad from 1952.* ■

## CLEMATIS STREET, MEET THE SHOPPING CENTERS

By the mid-'40s, the remodeled McCrory's was a landmark on Clematis Street (it had opened in 1914) and Burdines had moved into the Hatch's department store building (the white Art Moderne building at the northwest corner of Olive and Clematis). In 1954, Belks moved into that building and Burdines moved down the street. Five years later, Clematis got some competition from the area's first "shopping center" — Palm Coast Plaza, just north of the Lake Worth line. The plaza's two big draws: Its parking spaces and its air-conditioning. In 1960, the Bazaar International shopping plaza (right) — with its distinctive tower — opened just north of the West Palm Beach line in Riviera Beach. ■

# Our city's sport: Baseball!

In the early years of West Palm Beach, the fire siren would reverberate through the city every Thursday at noon. Stores would close so everyone could hit the beach — or attend the baseball games of the East Coast League, with teams made up of local businessmen.

By 1927 merchants could no longer afford that luxury — but baseball remained the city's favorite sport.

In the 1920s, the town hosted major league teams like the Baltimore Orioles, Cincinnati Reds and the New York Yankees (including the legendary Babe Ruth).

Spring training came to West Palm Beach when the St. Louis Browns, now the Baltimore Orioles, set up on March 3, 1928. The Philadelphia — later Kansas City — Athletics, managed by the great Connie Mack, trained from 1945 to 1962.

The Municipal Athletic Field, opened in 1924, was renamed Wright Field three years later, and Connie Mack Field in 1961. Today, Connie Mack Field is gone — replaced by the Kravis Center for the Performing Arts. But a marker in the parking garage is a lasting reminder of those good old baseball days.

WEST PALM BEACH'S TEAM, 1908

*This team "terrorized the lower east coast back in 1908," according to a news-paper caption from the '20s. Hardware store owner M.E. Gruber (center, in white) was the manager. Bob Baker (back row, third from left) would later become sheriff (see Page 93).* ■

## CONGRATULATIONS, MR. MACK

*Jerry and Jimmy Browning were 7 back in 1946, when their mother, Caroline, got a call from Bob Balfe, long-time sports editor of* The Palm Beach Post *and* Times. *There was a ceremony at Connie Mack Field to commemorate Mack's 50th year in baseball, and "they asked me to get my twins, dress them in a baseball hat, a football shirt and dungarees so they could pose as playground representatives for all the kids in West Palm Beach,"  Caroline Browning recalls. Jimmy was around the corner at a friend's house — so Jerry got the spotlight all to himself.* ∎

# The black leagues: "A glorious time"

*WEST PALM BEACH YANKEES, MID-1940s Johnny Williams (stooping, right) played with the team from 1944 to 1946, the same years they were Florida state champs in the black league. In 1948, the team was renamed the West Palm Beach Rockets, and they played teams in Cuba and Florida, said Williams, who was known as the Rockets' home-run king.* ■

At the turn of the century, black employees of the Royal Poinciana Hotel and The Breakers faced off in baseball games on Palm Beach to entertain winter guests. Many were hired for their baseball skills.

When the National Negro League began play in 1918, the West Palm Beach Giants and West Palm Beach Yankees played "pickup games" at Lincoln Park, now Coleman Park, along Lake Mangonia.

They would pay black youngsters 50 cents to distribute flyers, and they held New Orleans-style game-day parades two hours before the first pitch.

Later, the big-time Negro League teams would combine spring training, barnstorming and recruiting in West Palm Beach. Some of their greats would eventually break the sport's color barrier: Jackie Robinson and Satchel Paige. Others, as great as they were, never would: Josh Gibson, who once hit a ball that landed two streets over from Lincoln Park.

"It was a glorious time," recalls Preston Tillman, founder of the Black Historical Preservation Society. "The guys would really put on shows after the games, and sometimes before, and see who could hit the most home runs. It was fun. As kids we were out there after people had gone home. We'd be watching them hit the balls."

West Palm Beach, Tillman said, was "an incubator" for great local players who went on to sign with the big teams: first baseman Paul Dukes; Willie "Hot Potato" Burns, who struck out many of the stars; center fielder Jess Lang, who played in all-star games across Florida and in Cuba and once played on Jackie Robinson's barnstorming all-star team of black major league players.

"I was a better outfielder than a hitter," Lang recalls. "I was mostly a defensive player. Pretty fast. The fastest men on the team always played center field."

Eventually, integration and its new opportunities for both black players and fans spelled the end of the Negro leagues — but not the memories.

WEST PALM STADIUM
By 1969, the stadium hosted
two teams for spring training
— the Milwaukee, later
Atlanta, Braves and the new
Montreal Expos. In 1994,
both teams were discussing
moves: the Braves to Jupiter
and the Expos to a site at 45th
Street and Military Trail. ■

# Hey, batter — watch that sand

When the Braves came to town, baseball moved from Connie Mack Field to a modern stadium in the middle of nowhere.

New England developer Lou Perini bought the Braves in 1947, three years before they moved from Boston to Milwaukee. In the late '50s, Perini also happened to be developing 6,000 acres of scrub west of West Palm Beach. The match was a natural.

Perini gave the city the land for a baseball stadium with the idea of the Braves and Red Sox training here. But the Sox couldn't get out of their contract in Arizona.

When the Braves arrived in 1963, the stadium — built for only $1 million — was in the final stages of construction.

"I remember hitting three or four home runs over left field in the old ball park," Braves great Henry Aaron recalls now. When the new facility opened, it looked "like a major league ball park."

It was one of the first buildings of any size west of downtown and was in the middle of nowhere; Perini had to build a road at his own cost.

With no trees or buildings, blowing sand blinded players.

"The wind would blow everything across the field," recalls Pete Skorput, the Braves spring training coordinator. "All the people had to duck beneath their seats."

A practice diamond was so rough players called it "Iwo Jima."

But for a young Braves ballplayer named Joe Torre, now manager of the St. Louis Cardinals, "It was a lot better than Waycross, Ga.," home of the Braves' minor league spring training camp. "It was a modern stadium. It was just very windy."

Undaunted, the Braves squared off on March 9, 1963, against the city's former tenants: the Kansas City Athletics, who had trained at Wright Field for 17 years before moving to Bradenton.

The Athletics won 3-0; the winning RBI off Braves ace Warren Spahn came from the bat of a local youngster who would gain baseball fame as well: Dick Howser.

DICK HOWSER
After a stellar career at Palm
Beach High (Class of 1954),
Florida State University, and
three major league teams,
Howser managed the New
York Yankees and the Kansas
City Royals and earned a
World Series ring. He died of
cancer in 1987 at age 51. He
used this bat, now in Palm
Beach High's museum, in the
major leagues. ■

# Do these faces look familiar?

### TOGETHER FOR 17 YEARS

*In the early '60s, Channel 5 developed a news team that lasted through the '70s — an unusual feat in broadcasting. Bill Gordon was news director, Tony Glenn did the weather and Buck Kinnaird, known for his wild jackets, did sports. "On the day I started in 1962, they handed me a still photo of Rocky Marciano on a polo pony and said, 'Here are your files. Good luck,' " remembers Kinnaird (pictured with Gordon in 1962). "You were a one-man band in those days. We'd have to hang our film on a clothes line to dry, and when it rained, we had no film. So, we talked a lot." Channel 5's first studio was in Palm Beach (at 5 Cocoanut Row). "It flooded every time we had a big rain," Kinnaird recalls. "I can remember Tony wading around with his pants rolled up. But it was beautiful. We enjoyed it." Gordon (shown, left, in 1970) died in 1984 at age 57. Glenn is now in Galveston, Texas. And Kinnaird does public relations in West Palm Beach.* ■

### ACTION NEWS CAR, MID-'60S

*As Buck Kinnaird recalls, "We had one car (Bill Gordon is driving here), but we put a '4' on it so people thought we had more. We put a phone in the car so people would think we could call different places. But the phone wasn't connected." This car was overturned in a 1970 labor riot at Spreen Volkswagen on Okeechobee Road, Kinnaird said.* ■

LET'S DANCE
with
Tony Glenn

## TREASURE ISLE

*Hosted by John Bartholomew Tucker, the game show was bankrolled by John D. MacArthur, who owned the Colonnades Hotel on Singer Island, where it was shot, as well as WEAT-TV, Channel 12, now WPEC-TV. Contestant couples dressed in swimming garb had to overcome obstacles to reach an island, where they solved a limerick.* ■

## LET'S DANCE

*Channel 5 weatherman Tony Glenn wore many hats — he was host of Opening Night at the Royal Poinciana, Whiz Kids and Let's Dance, a teen dance party broadcast from venues such as bowling alleys, shopping centers and car dealerships.* ■

# A wide world in a little box

WPTV, ON THE AIR

*For the first time, Aug. 22, 1954, as WJNO; renamed WPTV in 1956.* ■

WEAT BECOMES WPEC

*Channel 12 switches call letters in 1974.* ■

The 1950s meant Howdy Doody and Davy Crockett. But first you had to have a TV station.

In the beginning, Florida had only two TV stations, in Miami and Jacksonville. WIRK-TV, Channel 21, signed on in West Palm Beach on Sept. 13, 1953, gambling that people would buy a $50 attachment to receive channels 14 to 83.

At the time, many people didn't even own sets, recalls Rome Hartman, an early WIRK partner: "Radio was king, and television had a long row to hoe before there were enough TVs in the market to make it a success."

That didn't stop stores from running page after page of ads for TV sets in *The Palm Beach Post* on the day the station went on the air.

Channel 21, broadcasting from the 12th floor of the Harvey building in downtown West Palm Beach, carried programs from the ABC, NBC, CBS and Dumont networks, each of which showed only a few programs a day. It broadcast grainy kinescopes mailed from New York, and shows might air a week late.

"We were really primitive," Hartman said.

Channels 5 and 12 started up in the next two years, and Channel 21 was gone by 1956; not enough people had bought the $50 gadgets.

Channel 5 called its early newscast *Five Star Final* — a concession to newspapers' monopoly on the news. In fact, early TV news was little more than a talking newspaper. Only still photographs were used, and any pictures brought in from around town were made with a Polaroid camera.

It wasn't until the early 1960s that stations began sending reporters into the field, nearly all of them shooting their own 16-millimeter film. Videotape didn't come along until the late 1970s.

Stations started giving newscasts dramatic names: *Newsarama, Dateline 90, Dateline 11.*

And the national television audience got one of its first looks at Palm Beach County with *Treasure Isle*, a game show broadcast for 13 weeks in 1968 from Singer Island.

# The Chillingworth murder: Racketeering and revenge

It may have been this area's crime of the century: the June 14, 1955, murder of Judge Curtis Eugene Chillingworth and his wife, Marjorie.

Chillingworth, born in 1896, was the son of West Palm Beach's first city attorney and grandson of its fifth mayor. In 1923, he became the youngest circuit judge in state history. By the '50s, he was one of the deans of Florida judges.

Along with State Attorney Phillip D. O'Connell and other officials, Chillingworth became suspicious of municipal Judge Joseph A. Peel's lavish lifestyle. They suspected Peel was protecting and taking part in gambling, moonshine and prostitution operations.

Among his alleged infractions: signing lawmen's search warrants, then, for a fee, tipping the intended targets. One raid after another turned up empty.

Two partners in Peel's racketeering were Floyd A. "Lucky" Holzapfel, an Oklahoman who'd worked on Peel's campaign for municipal judge, and George D. "Bobby" Lincoln, who ran pool halls, a taxi fleet, moonshine and numbers and was considered "boss" of his black Riviera Beach neighborhood.

On June 14, 1955, the Chillingworths were abducted from their summer beach house in Manalapan. Blood stains dotted a wooden stair leading to the beach. The couple was never found.

Soon after, Peel was forced to step down as judge and briefly disbarred for his handling of a divorce. Suddenly, raids began succeeding.

Little by little, Peel's shady ways began surfacing. A year later, his law partner survived a brutal beating and identified his attacker as Holzapfel. Suspicion of Peel, Holzapfel and Lincoln escalated.

In a Melbourne hotel room, a hidden microphone caught "Lucky" bragging of the murders.

He and Lincoln, he said, had slipped behind Chillingworth's beach house in a small motorboat just before midnight and pounded on the door, waking the two. They'd been told the judge's wife wouldn't be there, but she was.

They then bound and gagged the two and led them to the boat. As they walked down the stairs, Mrs. Chillingworth worked loose her gag and

*THE VICTIMS*
*Judge Curtis Eugene*
*Chillingworth and his*
*wife, Marjorie*
*Croude McKinley*
*Chillingworth.* ■

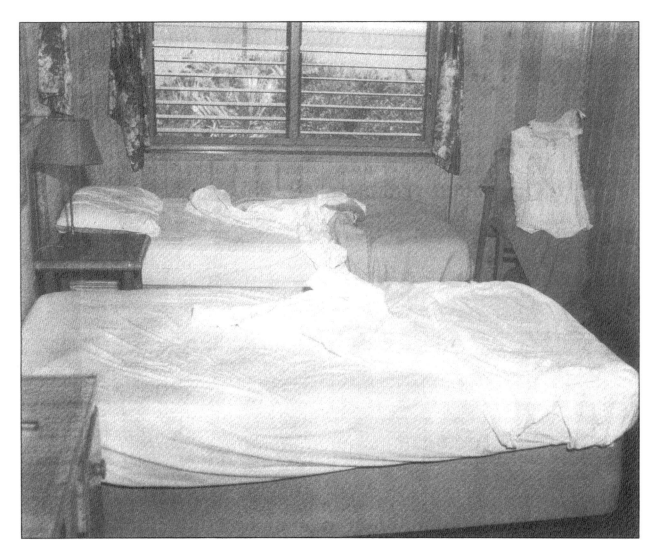

## THE CRIME SCENE
Snatched from their beds in their Manalapan beach house (above), the Chillingworths were bound and gagged and taken down wooden stairs to a boat. Blood was found on the stairs (left). As they were pushed overboard, they shouted their last words of love to each other. ∎

screamed, and Holzapfel struck her with his pistol, drawing blood.

The men headed out to sea, weighed the couple down and pushed them over as the two shouted their love for each other. When Chillingworth managed to stay afloat, they beat him and tied an anchor to his neck. Finally, he disappeared beneath the waves. Lucky called Peel and gave the prearranged code phrase: "I fixed that motor."

Later, it turned out Peel had told Holzapfel to kill O'Connell, then ordered a crony to take out Holzapfel, his "loose end."

Peel disappeared but was caught in Tennessee. He asked for immunity. The state attorney said no. Lincoln did agree to a deal. Holzapfel later pleaded guilty to two counts of capital murder. He was sent to prison for life. (Lincoln went to federal prison on unrelated moonshining charges until 1962.)

Peel's case was a local sensation and his trial had to be moved to Fort Pierce. On the stand, Holzapfel said, "We did it for Joe." A friend said Peel told him, "It was either that S.O.B. (Chillingworth) or me."

On March 30, 1961, after five-and-a-half hours, the jury found Peel guilty. He escaped the electric chair but went to prison for life. Paroled in 1979, he was immediately sent to federal prison to serve a stock fraud conviction, then was released in 1982 because he was dying of cancer. Nine days later, he confessed only to knowing about the crime and not preventing it, and went to the grave unyielding.

*THE PERPETRATORS — AND THE PUBLIC INTRIGUE*
*Municipal Judge Joseph Peel (top, right) was convicted of hiring Lucky Holzapfel (bottom) and Bobby Lincoln to kill the Chillingworths. The trial was so sensational it was moved to Fort Pierce, where people lined up to watch (right).* ■

# What I remember . . .

"**E**very Saturday morning, everybody who could get there would meet at Liggett's drugstore downtown. You'd buy a nickel soda and spend the morning bragging about what you did (the night before)."
— *Edward Eissey, Palm Beach High Class of 1946, and now president of Palm Beach Community College.*

"**W**hen I was in 11th grade, my dad and I were in a little garden store and the owner gave me my first orchid — a cattleya, white with a yellow throat. I still have offshoots from that first orchid. I got my love for the farmers in the Glades from my dad. He was the county agricultural agent, and he'd take me out into the fields when I was a bitty kid."
— *Circuit Judge Marvin Mounts, Class of 1950, Palm Beach High. Mounts Botanical Garden is named for his father, Red Mounts.*

"**I** loved the fruit juices and the coconut milk shakes at Sonny Boy's Fruit Stand. They'd mix orange juice or pineapple juice and coconut milk together — it was like an early piña colada. They had slot machines there, too. One day I had 5 cents left from my breakfast money, and I had to choose between getting a great big glass of orange juice or playing the slot machine, and I lost that nickel!"
— *Dora Digby, shown here at Sonny Boy's, which was on the southeast corner of Dixie and Belvedere, standing behind her friend Ann Bailey.*

"The highlight of the sixth grade at Military Trail Elementary was winding the maypole on May 1. We played hopscotch and jacks — we didn't have any cares in the world. In my sixth-grade picture (taken in 1953), I'm sixth from the left in the second row, next to our teacher, Mrs. Horne. John McLemore (second from right, top row) was the first boy who ever kissed me. We lived off of Military Trail by Southern Boulevard — which was way out west at that time. When I went to Palm Beach High, everyone used to tease me, 'Did you catch an alligator on your way to school today?' And you know where they live now? Wellington! So, now I tease them."

— *Mildred Smith Gruner, Class of '59, Palm Beach High, who now lives in Palm Beach Gardens.*

## Most likely to succeed

"It was a wonderful and happy time and a very influential period in my life."

— *Burt Reynolds, Class of 1954, Palm Beach High School.*

*Burt Reynolds, 1954*

Actor Reynolds is Palm Beach High's best-known graduate, but all three high schools had their share of notable students. Fellow actors Monte Markham (president of the Class of '53) and George Hamilton (Class of '57 — but he didn't graduate) also attended. Other prominent grads include Adrian Rogers (president of the Class of 1950), head of the Southern Baptist Convention, and two former presidents of the University of Florida — Marshall Criser (Class of '46) and Stephen O'Connell (Class of '34). Among Industrial High's famous grads are the Rev. Cecil Murray, pastor of the First AME Church in Los Angeles, who played a large role in calming the L.A. riots in 1993, and the Honorable Charlie J. Harrison, mayor of Pontiac, Mich. Actress Bhetty Waldron, co-founder of West Palm Beach's Quest Theatre, is a Roosevelt grad.

A SWINGING PROMOTIONAL BROCHURE, 1968
*"The SWING is to Palm Beach County . . . where the ACTION is"*
*touts this brochure from the Palm Beach County Development Board.*
*No doubt, the county and West Palm Beach were growing, as more and*
*more land became drained and developed to the west. The selling points:*
*condos, culture and, of course, the climate.* ■

Homes in Palm Beach County are designed to take a
of the mild, sunny climate by combining comfortab
facilities with outdoor living accommodations includi
ming pools and patios. There are many fine resider
ranging from inexpensive homes to luxury Country
munities. Lovely garden apartments, multiple family
and condominiums are available on waterfront site
dential areas and midtown locations.

## THE SWING IS TO PALM BEACH COUNTY TO *Live!*

Living in Palm Beach County means so much more than just packing
away your winter clothes. It means healthy living for every member of
the family. A climate that invites you out into the sun and surf, or golf
course, nearly every day of the year. You'll enjoy immaculate neighborhoods, lovely homes and apartments, superb shopping, churches of all
faiths, schools, parks, hospitals and modern medical centers.

Palm Beach County's edu-
cational picture is one
of continuing progress.
All schools are fully
accredited and include an
excellent parochial sys-
tem. Palm Beach Junior
College, Florida Atlantic
University, and a new
Baptist-sponsored college
are centers of higher
education.

Palm Beach County has a
total of 21 Catholic Churches,
265 Protestant, 5 Jewish
synagogues and 1 Mormon
Church.

In the Palm Beach Mall, you can shop among 87 different stores completely air conditioned and enclosed under one roof.

Cultural activities are varied and plentiful in Palm Beach County. There are 3 museums, 2 art galleries, 23 cultural societies, and 14 libraries. West Palm Beach's modern Municipal Library and the Science Museum and Planetarium are dedicated to the pursuit of knowledge.

✺

# *Chapter 10*

# The Mall & The Sprawl

## 1963-1980

*"It's sand castles instead of mud pies for this little girl. She breathes fresh, clean air for there is no metropolitan pollution. She doesn't just exist ... she lives! Sound good? You bet it's good. Palm Beach County could be your future. Clean blue-chip industry, big industrial parks, clean jobs ... a new, uncomplicated way of life."*

— Palm Beach County Development Board
advertisement, November 1969

How simple it all seemed. But life in West Palm Beach wasn't really so uncomplicated.

In the late '60s and the '70s, the city changed from a small town centered around downtown to a sprawling metropolis — with a host of new urban problems. Though the city's second boom had begun in the '50s, the city's new identity didn't emerge until a decade later. It was tied dramatically to one developer: Louis Perini.

Perini developed miles of swampland west of downtown, and by 1970, Palm Beach Lakes Boulevard and the Palm Beach Mall were challenging Clematis Street for shopping supremacy. When Interstate 95 was built — conveniently right through Perini's property — West Palm Beach was changed forever.

Big industry — Pratt & Whitney, IBM, RCA and others — helped put the city on the map. But now the focus was on the whole of Palm Beach County, not just West Palm Beach. The city was losing its position as the county's hub and heart.

And so many other things were changing.

Integration brought the end of Palm Beach and Roosevelt high schools and the beginning of a new high school, Twin Lakes.

The Vietnam War prompted young people to protest the conflict — and proclaim peace and free love. The Palm Beach International Raceway hosted a music festival to rival Woodstock.

And soon, the last bastions of the carefree days — The Hut and the Campus Shop — would serve their final meals.

# Key events: 1963-1980

**Aug. 27, 1964:** Hurricane Cleo causes $50 million damage in Palm Beach County.

**Sept. 14, 1964:** Florida Atlantic University opens in Boca Raton.

*Palm Beach International Airport.*

**Oct. 14, 1964:** Hurricane Isbell crosses Everglades from west and strikes area, causing about $700,000 damage.

**June 4, 1965:** Roosevelt Junior College for blacks becomes branch of Palm Beach Junior College and closes.

**Sept. 7-8, 1965:** Hurricane Betsy's outer edge causes scattered damage to Palm Beach County as it passes through Florida Keys.

**December 1965:** New city police headquarters, jail and court complex open at 901 Datura St.

**Feb. 7, 1966:** City commission votes to end segregation of city's cemeteries.

**Oct. 4, 1966:** WTVX-TV, Channel 34 in Fort Pierce, becomes the Palm Beach County/Treasure Coast CBS affiliate.

**Oct. 29, 1966:** New five-building terminal dedicated at Palm Beach International Airport.

**Dec. 14, 1966:** First portion of Interstate 95 in Palm Beach County, a 3.6-mile stretch from Okeechobee Boulevard to 45th Street, opens. Expressway completed north to Palm Beach Gardens in 1969.

**July 30-Aug. 1, 1967:** One night after 4-hour riot in adjacent Riviera Beach, scattered gangs set fires, smash windows and shoot at police in West Palm Beach.

**Aug. 20, 1967:** Lion Country Safari, a 659-acre jungle park, opens 15 miles west of West Palm Beach off Southern Boulevard. It will host about a half-million people a year.

*Lion Country Safari.*

**September 1967:** IBM opens in Boca Raton.

**Sept. 3, 1967:** West Palm Beach Auditorium opens.

**Oct. 26, 1967:** Palm Beach Mall opens with 87 stores and Gov. Claude Kirk presiding.

**September 1968:** Palm Beach Atlantic College opens in downtown West Palm Beach with 88 students.

*Landfill widens Flagler Drive.*

**June 9, 1969:** Officials open newly configured Flagler Drive after three-year, $800,000 "Cove Project;" waterway filled between Lakeview and First, and Flagler widened from two to four lanes.

**Nov. 28-30, 1969:** Palm Beach International Music and Arts Festival draws 40,000 to Palm Beach International Speedway.

**1970:** Population: Florida 6,791,418; Palm Beach County 348,993, West Palm Beach 57,375.

**May 4, 1970:** *The Palm Beach Post* is awarded a Pulitzer Prize in feature photography for its photographs of the poverty and poor working conditions of farm workers in the Glades.

**Fall 1970:** Palm Beach High and Roosevelt High combine into Twin Lakes. The Roosevelt High campus eventually becomes a middle school.

**November 1971:** Scientists find the first cases on the South Florida mainland of lethal yellowing, a plant disease that nearly wipes out Palm Beach County's namesake coconut palms.

**Feb. 17, 1972:** Palm Beach County Commission approves the first planned unit development for a far-flung 7,400-acre tract that will become Wellington.

**Jan. 27, 1974:** WEAT-TV, Channel 12, becomes WPEC-TV.

**July 3, 1976:** Interstate 95 is completed between Palm Beach Gardens and Miami.

**Jan. 20, 1977:** First-ever recorded snow in West Palm Beach. Most flakes melt on impact.

**1978:** Main post office, at Olive Avenue and Fern Street for nearly four decades before closing in December 1972, is demolished.

**Jan. 6, 1978:** John D. MacArthur, the billionaire who bought much of the undeveloped land in northern Palm Beach and southern Martin counties and founded the city of Palm Beach Gardens, dies.

**March 28, 1978:** After the city begins electing commissioners by district rather than at large, Eva Mack and Ruby L. Bullock are the first blacks elected to city commission. Commissioners elect Helen Wilkes as the first woman mayor.

**May 31, 1979:** Library's new basement section opens; inventory increases by more than 50,000 books.

**Sept. 3, 1979:** Hurricane David, after leaving more than 1,000 dead in the Caribbean, slides up Palm Beach County coast, collapsing Palm Beach Jai Alai roof and WJNO Radio tower, and leaves about $30 million damage. It then causes destruction along Space Coast and northeast Florida. Five are killed in state.

# Up from swamp and marsh:

# Perini's "Westward Expansion"

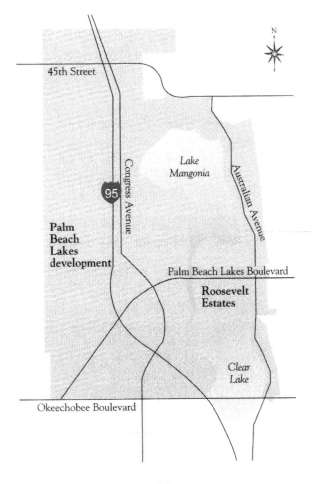

**PALM BEACH LAKES**
*Louis Perini's development, as shown on a 1994 base map. That land purchase now accounts for a third of the city's size.* ■

In the mid-1950s, West Palm Beach was only a mile wide. But a single land deal set off a westward land rush now limited only by sugar fields and the Everglades.

It started with a 1951 study on potential for westward growth.

"The city was stagnated and bursting at its seams," former city attorney Grover Herring said in 1977.

The West Palm Beach Water Company, still owned by Flagler interests, had a monopoly both on the city's water supply and some 17,000 acres, nearly 27 square miles of land and marsh west of the city.

The city's primitive sewer system, which served 60 percent of the residents — the rest used septic tanks — dumped its raw effluent into the Intracoastal Waterway. A polio outbreak spurred the city into action.

It floated a bond for the titanic sum of $18 million and, in 1955, installed an upgraded city sewer system and bought the water plant and the western land.

Eventually all that land would be annexed into the city. About 21.75 square miles became the city's water catchment area.

In 1957, the city sold off the remaining 5,500 acres to five investors for $4.35 million.

That property now is roughly bounded by 45th Street, Okeechobee Boulevard, Australian Avenue and a line about a half-mile east of Military Trail.

The "Westward Expansion" became one of the state's first planned community developments.

Much of that land was under water. About 30 million cubic yards of fill was moved, converting swamp into dry land and enlarging and deepening the lakes.

No one worried about wetlands protection then.

It was a boon for blacks, many of whom had moved to Riviera Beach after their segregated neighborhoods ran out of room.

In fact, the first development was Roosevelt Estates, which became a major moderate income neighborhood for black families.

But within two years, the consortium realized it was

financially in over its head. The partners sold out, leaving Massachusetts developer Louis R. Perini Sr., then also the owner of the Milwaukee (later Atlanta) Braves.

Perini also had trouble finding backers.

"For years people thought we were fools," John Linstroth, Perini Land and Development president, said in 1982. "Some Perini executives said for years that their bonuses were sunk in Florida."

But eventually the development grew. Interstate 95 opened right through the development. Roads were extended west from downtown. Soon came Palm Beach Mall, the Forum business complexes, the city auditorium and stadium, the Ramada Inn hotel, the Land of the Presidents golf course, the 7,300-unit Villages of Palm Beach Lakes and other developments.

Perini died in 1972; he wouldn't recognize the place now.

"West Palm Beach would be just a non-entity today if not for that development," Herring recalls now. "There is no developer that could have done what Perini did. Had this not been done at that particular time it would have been impossible to do it later because of all the environmental laws."

## "CITY WITHIN A CITY"

*To sell his company's new development, Perini built a hyperbolic paraboloid to serve as hub of its "Million Dollar Homes Exhibit." This brochure touted the Palm Beach Lakes development as "Tomorrow-ness in action." The star-shaped building, at Okeechobee Road and Florida Mango Road, was gone by the mid-1960s.* ∎

*Palm Beach Mall, height of chic shopping in 1968.*

*West Palm Beach's big top, 1970.*

In 1967, residents found two new reasons to drive to Palm Beach Lakes Boulevard: the West Palm Beach auditorium and the Palm Beach Mall.

Critics dubbed the 7,000-seat auditorium "the leaky tepee" when leaks sprang the first year.

Carnegie Hall it wasn't. The moat cracked. A flying pulley hit a violinist. Chirping birds competed with musicians. Balladeer Jimmy Buffett said the place was too filthy even for him.

In 1983, new managers cleaned up the auditorium and refilled the moat with water.

The Palm Beach Mall, with 87 stores including Jordan Marsh, Richard's and J.C. Penney, was advertised as "a million square feet all under one roof."

In 1979, it gained a new tenant — Burdines, an institution downtown for more than 35 years. Sears, then on Dixie Highway, followed in 1980.

# . . . and Century Village

In the '60s, West Palm Beach learned a new, important word: Condominium.

It means "common ownership" — and it also meant a bonanza for developers. Instead of paying $400,000 for 400 feet of oceanfront and building one or two homes, they could plant a 100-unit tower.

And then came another kind of condo complex: Century Village.

The concept was revolutionary. Retirees could flee their old brownstones and walkups and live the good life — in apartments that cost just $10,000 or $15,000 each.

The 683-acre development at Florida's Turnpike and Okeechobee Boulevard started as a mobile home park in January 1969; by 1974, it was a 7,854-unit sprawling community. Three more Century Villages would open, in Boca Raton and in southern and northern Broward County. In the season, about 15,000 people live at the West Palm Beach site alone.

They entertain themselves with a 1,000-seat auditorium, a "party room," and, of course, shuffleboard.

And they flex strong political muscle. The community is more than 75 percent Jewish, heavily from the northeast and Canada, and traditionally votes Democratic and liberal. At election time, the block vote of Century Village residents is never ignored.

*"A WAY OF LIFE"*
*State Rep. Ray Moudry, spokesman Red Buttons, Century Village developer H. Irwin Levy and State Sen. Tom Johnson break ground on a Century Village expansion in 1971 (top, right). Levy's concept of Century Village was "to provide a way of life, more than just housing."* ■

# Trouble on Main Street

In the early '70s, coming downtown remained a routine. The bus dropped customers off right outside of Kress's (above), and going to Burdines (with its lunch counter) was a special treat. But Clematis Street was in trouble. In 1979, Burdines closed its downtown store (below) and moved to the Palm Beach Mall — and the social habit of spending the day shopping and strolling moved right along with it. As early as 1976, 40 percent of downtown retail buildings were empty, and downtown's contribution to the city tax base had dropped from 20 percent to 8 percent. ■

# Integration: "The time has come"

"We knew segregation was wrong, but some things you do and wait for your time," says Alice Moore, who grew up in the city's Northwest neighborhood and went to Industrial High School. "In the early '60s, we said, 'The time has come to invoke a peaceful integration.'"

An interracial group of women — the Church Women United — decided to go to the movies on a Saturday night, Moore recalls. The black women sat down next to the white women — not in the balcony, as they had done before.

"And then we went to Burdines and Woolworth's and did the same thing," Moore recalls.

But not all the city's race relations were so peaceful.

Things got hot in the hot summer of 1967. After a four-hour disturbance on July 30, in Riviera Beach, scattered gangs rampaged the next night in West Palm Beach, smashing windows, setting fires and shooting at police.

No one was hurt, but Gov. Claude Kirk threatened to slap a curfew on the city. Things quickly calmed.

NO MORE PALM BEACH HIGH
*When school started in the fall of 1970, there was no more Palm Beach High School or Roosevelt High School. They were combined into "Twin Lakes," and this sign at Palm Beach High was taped over.* ■

# The birth of Twin Lakes

*"A DIFFICULT YEAR"*

*The first year at Twin Lakes was "very, very difficult," recalls Bettye Tanner Dawson, who had taught English at Roosevelt High School. "Some students were taught on the Roosevelt campus (called Twin Lakes North, above) and part were taught at the old Palm Beach High (called Twin Lakes South, facing page)."* ■

West Palm Beach lawyer William Holland helped open the doors to the schoolhouse.

In September 1956, two years after the landmark U.S. Supreme Court ruling in Brown vs. Board of Education, Holland sued to have his son, William Jr., attend a white school.

"We put a lot of pain and bloodshed" into those early battles, Holland, whose Lake Park home was bombed twice and vandalized several times, recalled in 1990.

"I remember when I was 6 or 7, he took me to one of the elementaries down there to be enrolled," William M. Holland Jr. recalls now. "I recall going there — and leaving."

One federal judge turned Holland down, but an appeals court said yes and ordered Palm Beach County to integrate its schools.

The district stalled and Florida Attorney General Richard W. Ervin urged every school board in the state to "exhaust every possible legal remedy" to avoid desegregation.

A handful of students attended white schools as early as 1961 and Holland's son finally entered in 1963.

Linda Hall, who was one of the first blacks to integrate Palm Beach High and who graduated in 1968, recalled that "boys lined the walkway and tried to burn us with cigarettes. They threatened us. The police stood on the side, and they were really very negative."

In 1969, the U.S. Supreme Court called for desegregation to begin "at once." The next year, it did.

"Hell no, mine won't go," white parents shouted at anti-integration rallies. Many put their kids in private schools.

Many blacks, while welcoming opportunity, didn't want to leave their black schools.

Across the county, fires were set. Police in riot gear broke up fights. A stick of dynamite was found on a bus. A student was slashed. One was dragged down a stair, another pushed through a window.

Beginning with the 1970-71 school year, Palm Beach High and Roosevelt High ceased to exist; the historic schools were combined into a new entity on the hill called Twin Lakes. Roosevelt eventually became a middle school.

## A NEW IDENTITY

"With the dawning of a new age, so dawns a new school . . ." reads the introduction to the 1971 yearbook, The Aquarian. *The yearbook caption with this photo of part of the first student council (left) says,* "What is the purpose of the student council? Maybe to bridge the gap between faculty and students . . . or to curb tension." ■

# Hey, man, is this Woodstock?

Janis Joplin was here. So were the Rolling Stones. And the Jefferson Airplane, Grand Funk Railroad, Iron Butterfly, Sly and the Family Stone — and 40,000 young people.

On the weekend of Nov. 28 to 30, 1969, the Palm Beach International Raceway (now Moroso Motorsports) hosted the Palm Beach International Music and Arts Festival. It happened three-and-a-half months after Woodstock and was considered "Woodstock South."

*The Palm Beach Post* quoted one "hippie" in attendance this way: "I mean, we are really freaking out in Vietnam. Who needs war, man, when you've got love . . . It's a real groove here. There's no hassle. The only hangups are the ones you come with."

Plus those three other hangups — rain, mud and police.

Sheriff William Heidtman's deputies arrested 114 people for drug sales, and 133 people were treated for overdoses or bad trips.

Heidtman, sheriff from 1967 to 1977 and a self-described "tough son of a bitch," admitted in 1989 that he had men plant red ants at the concert site and lure alligators into canals where people were swimming. "I had to do what I had to do to get them to know they weren't going to run the show — we were."

The police also got tough the next year to clean out the hippie element at "People's Park," a grassy area just north of Phillips Point.

The park "was a damned national disgrace," Police Chief William Barnes said later. "Pot smoking, hell-raising, fornicating on the grounds, bottle and rock throwing — you name it."

On July 7, 1970, city workers began posting "keep off signs" — and 64 people were arrested at People's Park. In 1972, the city ordered parks closed at 9 p.m. — ending the hippies' hold on the park.

## COVERAGE AS THICK AS THE MUD

The Palm Beach Post devoted most of its front page for three days to the rock festival. One story tried to explain the hippie mentality: "The world is an uncomfortable place to the hippie sometimes . . . Most of the hippies are warm people when they accept you into their circles . . . They claim to be persecuted by those who don't take the time to understand." ■

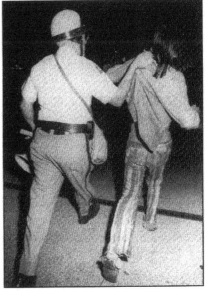

PEACE AND LOVE
. . . SORT OF
"Woodstock South" at the
Palm Beach International
Raceway attracted these fans
(left, top and bottom), who
braved rain, mud and cold to
groove to the music in 1969.
In 1970, police were called
in to clear out "People's
Park," a hippie hangout just
north of Phillips Point
(above). ■

# West Palm's three Florida Senate presidents

State Sen. Phil Lewis (right) leans over to confer with fellow senator Harry A. Johnston II, also of West Palm Beach, in the late '70s. ■

Jerry Thomas, 1977. ■

From the mid-'60s through the mid-'80s, Florida politics was dominated by three childhood friends from West Palm Beach: Jerry Thomas, Phil Lewis and Harry Johnston II.

Thomas, born and bred in West Palm Beach, was senate president in 1971-72. He was known as "Mr. Conservation" and was instrumental in stopping the dumping of inadequately treated sewage into Lake Worth. He was author or co-sponsor of hundreds of laws, including the Florida Sunshine Law.

"Jerry Thomas probably was the most significant environmental law changer in the history of this state," Lewis said. "He was years ahead of everybody else."

Thomas encouraged his friend Lewis, who had come to West Palm Beach when he was 3, to get into politics.

"When I ran (for Florida Senate) in 1970, I took on the interstate. From Okeechobee to Southern boulevards was the worst link in the interstate system," he recalled in 1994. "Harry Johnston's papa, Col. Johnston, who helped make history every day he was here, set aside the right of way for I-95, yet we were the last section built. We had public hearings for 22 months and made it happen. Today, you can drive down to Delray for lunch, but in those days you wouldn't have thought about doing that unless you had a gun to your head."

Lewis was president of the state senate for the '79-'80 session. And Harry A. Johnston II (the son of Col. Johnston, a veteran of both world wars and the county's attorney for 35 years) was senate president in 1985-86.

Today, Johnston is a U.S. congressman and Lewis runs a real estate business in Riviera Beach. Thomas died of cancer in 1980 at the age of 51. At his memorial service, Lewis called him "a man for all seasons." Today, the bridge from Riviera Beach to Singer Island and an elementary school in Jupiter are named for Jerry Thomas.

# What I remember . . .

"The thing I miss most is the brownies at the Campus Shop. They were the best in the world. I'd give $1,000 now for that brownie recipe."

— *John Rice, Class of 1969, Palm Beach High.*

"In the early '60s, integration was coming, and everyone was apprehensive. Lake Lytal was probably one of the best county commissioners we ever had. He was real smart and knew how to handle people. At that time in the courthouse, the drinking fountains were labeled 'white' and 'colored.' One weekend, Lytal brought in county work crews to paint out the signs. When everyone came to work on Monday, this miraculous change had occurred."

— *Circuit Judge Marvin Mounts, a West Palm Beach native.*

"I don't think people look at gender and race now (1994). I think they look at the qualifications of the people running for office. In my time, blacks had no choice."

*— Eva Mack, named the city's first black mayor in 1982.*
*For West Palm Beach's first half century, its city commission was all white and male. In April 1949, Estelle Murer was elected the city's first woman commissioner. It would be 26 years before the next one, Carol Roberts, was elected in March 1975. Three years later, in March 1978, Mack and Ruby L. Bullock became the first blacks elected to the city commission. That same year, the commission named Helen Wilkes the first woman mayor.*

*Greg and John Rice, who graduated from Palm Beach High in 1969.* ■

*Eva Mack (left) and Ruby Bullock accept greetings from friends after being sworn in as West Palm Beach's first black commissioners in March 1978.* ■

WEST PALM BEACH WATERFRONT, 1993
*Nine high-rises sprang up from 1978 to 1989, but behind the growth lurked problems, especially crime. Serious crime rose 25 percent between 1984 and 1985, and the city found itself first among the nation's medium-sized cities in serious crime. It stayed near the top for several years.*

## Chapter 11

# Rethinking the Heart of the City

### 1980-1994

Glass skyscrapers cluster along the waterfront — but the city's people do not.

As West Palm Beach heads into its next 100 years, the challenge is clear: Can the city's heart — downtown — be renewed? Can West Palm Beach revive the pioneering spirit so alive a century ago?

The city's economic decline, begun as early as the 1970s, brought with it urban decay and crime. Though Palm Beach County's population more than doubled between 1970 and 1990, West Palm Beach grew at a slower pace (in 1993, with a population of 64,818, Boca Raton was almost as big as West Palm Beach, population 68,000). And Okeechobee Boulevard, gateway to Interstate 95, allowed people to get in and out of town — fast.

But it wasn't all bad news. From 1979 to 1982, the city approved plans for six high-rises, more growth than downtown had seen in five decades.

And by 1991, a "strong mayor" system of government brought new hope.

Nancy Graham was the city's first elected mayor in seven decades and its first "strong mayor," with authority over the city manager, the power to hire and fire department heads, and the job of preparing the budget.

Graham's platform included an $18 million bond issue for revitalizing downtown, including $4 million for the waterfront alone and a major facelift of the city library.

The bond passed, and a prestigious South Florida planning firm presented a bold master plan that was clear on what downtown should *not* be: a giant city inhabited by high-rises. And what it *should* be: a place where people don't just work, but where they also live and shop and play.

To usher in 1994, 20,000 partiers came downtown to celebrate the implosion of the decrepit Holiday Inn. The 33-year-old hotel at Datura and Narcissus streets, empty since 1986 and a haven for the homeless, had become a metaphor for the decaying downtown.

In its place, an outdoor band shell is being built, with an expanse of grass and a sparkling view of Lake Worth — the same view pioneers once traveled long days and nights to see.

It will be a City Park — much like the one Henry Flagler first dreamed of 100 years ago.

# Key events: 1980-1994

**1980:** Population: Florida 9,746,324, Palm Beach County 576,812, West Palm Beach 63,305.

**Jan. 14, 1980:** New City Hall opens at Dixie Highway and Second Street.

**Sept. 12, 1980:** Commuter plane from West Palm Beach to Freeport, Grand Bahama, crashes into the ocean, killing all 34 aboard. It is the only major air crash involving Palm Beach International Airport.

**May 1, 1981:** City jail closes. All prisoners go to county jail.

**July 1981:** Former City Hall on Second Street razed for a parking garage

**July 8, 1982:** Public station WWPF-TV, Channel 42, signs on. It later changes name to WHRS and becomes WXEL Jan. 1, 1985.

**October 1982:** Independent station WFLX-TV, Channel 29, signs on.

**Dec. 1, 1982:** New sheriff's office and jail opens on Gun Club Road, south of airport.

**May 6-15, 1983:** The first SunFest, replacing the Royal Palm Arts Festival, draws about 100,000 to Flagler Drive.

**March 22, 1984:** New county governmental center opens adjacent to county courthouse.

**November 1986:** New $25 million main post office opens on Summit Boulevard.

**May 4, 1987:** *The Evening Times* merges with sister paper *The Palm Beach Post*; afternoon edition of *The Post* carries both mastheads.

**Sept. 25, 1987:** Last newspaper bearing double mastheads of *The Palm Beach Post* and *The Evening Times* published; *The Times* officially ceases publication.

**Dec. 19, 1987:** "Missing link" of Interstate 95, from Palm Beach Gardens to Stuart, opens, completing expressway from Miami to Maine.

**April 16, 1988:** Area code 407 established from Boca Raton to Orlando.

**May 31, 1988:** City annexes about 1,500 acres near Beeline Highway, slated for upscale homes and a garbage burning plant.

**June 1, 1988:** Twin Lakes High School, the former Palm Beach High, graduates its last class.

**June 15, 1988:** Palm Beach Junior College renamed Palm Beach Community College.

**Sept. 13, 1988:** Palm Beach Lakes High School, successor to Twin Lakes, opens in the old school building; the new Palm Beach Lakes building opens Jan. 30, 1989.

**Sept. 19, 1988:** WAQ-TV, Channel 19 (independent), signs on.

*Palm Beach International Airport.*

**Oct. 24, 1988:** New passenger terminal and parking garage opened at PBIA; named for World War II ace David McCampbell.

**Jan. 1, 1989:** WPEC-TV, Channel 12, switches from ABC to CBS; WPBF-TV, Channel 25, signs on as ABC affiliate; and former CBS affiliate WTVX-TV, Channel 34, becomes an independent.

**Jan. 9, 1989:** Tri-Rail commuter train, a 70-mile line from West Palm Beach to Miami, begins service.

**Nov. 6, 1989:** City changes First Street, formerly Banyan Street, to Banyan Boulevard.

**1990:** Population: Florida 12,937,926; Palm Beach County 863,518; West Palm Beach 67,643.

*New Palm Beach County Courthouse.*

**Feb. 7, 1990:** County commissioners approve $260 million in bonds to build a $125-million, 11-story, block-long courthouse and to improve the county jail. The new courthouse is scheduled to open in October 1994.

**April 1991:** A Jupiter woman, Patricia Bowman, accuses William Kennedy Smith (nephew of the late President John F. Kennedy) of raping her March 30 behind the Kennedy estate in Palm Beach. The trial in Palm Beach Circuit Court lures world press to downtown West Palm Beach. Smith is acquitted on Dec. 11, 1991.

**Oct. 20, 1991:** Abandoned burial ground behind Tamarind Avenue home, believed to contain about 674 black victims of 1928 hurricane, is rededicated.

**Nov. 19, 1991:** Nancy Graham becomes city's first elected mayor in seven decades.

**March 1992:** Ground broken for new $18 million city police station at 600 Banyan Blvd., set to open in early 1995.

**May 9, 1992:** Norton Gallery of Art reveals 10-year expansion plan that will include a new building, doubling the facility's space.

**Fall 1992:** Palm Beach County manages relief effort for southern Dade County, ravaged by Hurricane Andrew.

**Sept. 19, 1992:** Raymond F. Kravis Center for the Performing Arts opens.

**Jan. 1, 1994:** Downtown Holiday Inn imploded; to be replaced by outdoor amphitheater.

**May 6, 1994:** City breaks ground for new $4 waterfront facelift, including remake of library.

**Nov. 5, 1994:** West Palm Beach celebrates its centennial.

*William Kennedy Smith with his mother Jean and aunts Ethel Kennedy and Eunice Shriver.*

# SunFest: What a show!

What the Sun Dance festival was to the '30s, SunFest is to the '90s: A great excuse for a springtime party along the waterfront.

The first SunFest in 1983 ran for 10 days and lost $120,000. But organizers wised up and packed everything into a long weekend. The festival's popularity took off — hampered only in 1988 when a storm washed out much of the weekend.

By the mid-1990s, SunFest was being headlined by national music acts, averaging about 300,000 fans a year, and running operating budgets of about $2 million.

*FIREWORKS FROM PHILLIPS POINT*
*Jim Carter and Grace Zopf watch the SunFest fireworks in May 1989 from the Phillips Point parking garage, while the throngs gather below.* ∎

# Downtown/Uptown: A great idea, but . . .

It was perhaps the greatest vision for downtown West Palm Beach since Henry Flagler laid it out. But, like so many other great ideas, Downtown/Uptown didn't happen.

Henry J. Rolfs Sr., a retired Virginia developer, and David C. Paladino Jr., developer by day and rock musician by night, envisioned "a grand gateway" west of downtown, which had become the domain of street-level criminals, crack addicts and the homeless.

They tore down about 77 acres of decaying homes and businesses and projected $33 million in construction over two decades — offices, stores, hotels, homes, parks — with the Kravis Center as a centerpiece.

But the project stalled. Soon a Finnish bank foreclosed on the 30 acres at the core of the project. Rolfs died in May 1994. In summer 1994, the fate of Downtown/Uptown remained in limbo.

*DEMOLITION WEST OF DOWNTOWN*
*Phillips Point and Esperanté office towers rise behind the rubble of Downtown/Uptown in 1990.* ■

*WHERE DOWNTOWN/UPTOWN WAS SUPPOSED TO BE*
*This 1988 aerial shows Okeechobee Boulevard (bottom of photo), Connie Mack Field (left), the Twin Lakes High School complex (center) and the area to the east and south of the high school that was to be developed for Downtown/Uptown. In 1992, the Raymond F. Kravis Center for the Performing Arts would rise on the Connie Mack Field site.* ■

RAYMOND F. KRAVIS CENTER FOR THE PERFORMING ARTS
*Home to Broadway shows, local performances and every type of act in
between, the Kravis Center was called "a little Lincoln Center" by actress
Elizabeth Ashley, who attended the gala opening in November 1992.*

# The Kravis Center: A shining star

"Is this a miracle or what?" Burt Reynolds asked at the November 1992 gala grand opening of West Palm Beach's cultural mecca on the hill, the Raymond F. Kravis Center for the Performing Arts.

The $63-million-plus performing arts center — a 2,189-seat auditorium, a 230-seat hall and an outdoor amphitheater for about 1,800 — was first envisioned in 1978 by WPEC-TV owner Alex Dreyfoos.

The site changed many times — first Currie Park, then Palm Beach Community College's main campus in Lake Worth, then it was to be the jewel of the ill-fated Downtown/Uptown project.

Through it all, Dreyfoos persisted. Finally, the center was built with money raised by public and private groups and individuals — many devoted to the center's namesake, Oklahoma oilman Raymond F. Kravis, who had wintered in Palm Beach for decades. Though some criticized the center as a publicly financed monument to high society in the middle of a decaying neighborhood, most agreed it was a triumph.

Indeed, the opening ceremonies were the best of both worlds: free entertainment for the public in September 1992 and a star-studded, $1,000-a-ticket gala in November hosted by favorite son Reynolds. *The Palm Beach Post* called it the "social event to end all social events."

## GUIDING LIGHTS

*Alexander Dreyfoos Jr. spearheaded the effort to build a stellar arts center in West Palm Beach. He poses with his wife, Carolyn, and the center's namesake, Raymond F. Kravis, in the spectacular lobby (left and above). Kravis died Oct. 25, 1993.* ■

## THE VISION

The master plan for West Palm Beach's revived waterfront features a clam-shaped band shell, amphitheater, children's museum, walkways for pedestrians and boat docks. Team Plan Inc. of North Palm Beach is the coordinating consultant on the waterfront project and Schwab, Twitty & Hanser Architectural Group is the firm handling the new library entrance. ■

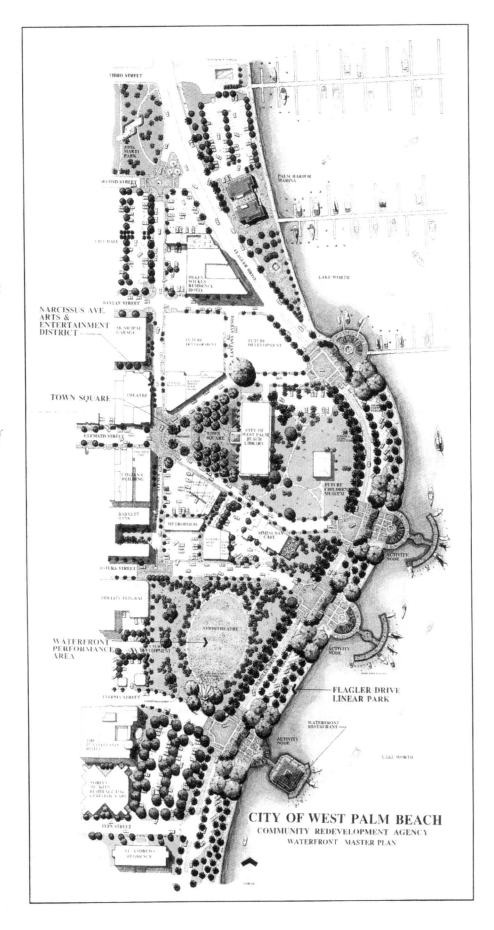

**CITY OF WEST PALM BEACH**
COMMUNITY REDEVELOPMENT AGENCY
WATERFRONT MASTER PLAN

# Nov. 5, 1994: Dawn of a new downtown?

*NEW FOUNTAIN The $750,000 triangular fountain in Town Square will shoot jets of water in patterns controlled by a computer. The library will be getting a facelift soon as well.* ■

When West Palm beach celebrates its centennial on Nov. 5, 1994, it also will be celebrating its new Town Square.

Narcissus Avenue will be rebuilt from Second Street to Datura Street, with new sidewalks to match the ones built on Clematis Street in 1993. A park and amphitheater will grace the waterfront. And a dancing fountain will anchor Town Square in front of the library. The library, too, is getting a new facade, though that will come later.

This is part of a dramatic $4 million waterfront renovation geared to bringing people back downtown. Some of the country's most noted architects contributed to the plan, including Dan Kiley of Vermont, who also designed the grounds for the Gateway Arch in St. Louis and the Lincoln Center in New York. Town Square fits into the people-friendly master plan for the city done in 1993 by Miami architects Andres Duany and Elizabeth Plater-Zyberk.

Nightclubs have already started lining Clematis Street, and some believe that West Palm Beach could become "North Beach" — a northern cousin to Miami's hip South Beach.

As Duany said in 1993, "The minute you have two decent blocks this will become a famous place."

*New signs on Clematis Street.*

# West Palm Beach Mayors

John S. Earman, 1894-1896. Publisher.

J.F. Lamond, 1896-1897. Express agent.

Marion E. Gruber, 1897-1898. Merchant.

Wilmon Whilldin, 1898-1899. Real estate.

R.J. Chillingworth, 1899-1901. Attorney.

George G. Currie, 1901-1902. Attorney.

L.W. Burkhardt, 1902. Grocer.

George G. Currie, 1902-1904.

W.I. Metcalf, 1904-1905. Publisher.

George B. Baker, 1905-1907. Sheriff.

J.T. DeBerry, 1907-1909. Ferry operator.

George W. Potter, 1909-1910. Lumber, real estate.

J.B. McGinley, 1910-1912. Merchant, real estate.

C.S. Anderson, 1912-1914. Profession unknown.

M.D. Carmichael, 1914-1916. Attorney.

W. A. Dutch, 1916-1920. Bonds, investor.

D.F. Dunkle, 1920-1921. Bonds, real estate.

M.D. Carmichael, 1921-1922.

L. Garland Biggers, 1922-1923. Real estate. Last elected mayor until 1991.

Joseph Mendel, 1923-1924. Cigar manufacturer.

Henry Stephen Harvey, 1924-1926. Architect.

Spencer T. Lainhart, 1926-1927. Building materials.

J.C. McCreary, 1927-1928. Pharmacist, postmaster.

Vincent Oaksmith, 1928-1930. Tobacconist, insurance agent.

John R. Beacham, 1930-1931. Attorney.

E.B. Donnell, 1931-1933. Attorney and judge.

Charles B. Watkins, 1933-1934. Bottled water dealer.

Paschal C. "Pat" Reese, 1934-1935. Attorney.

F. Theodore "Ted" Brown, 1935-1937. Real estate.

S.D. "Sam" Morris, 1937-1939. Real estate.

Ernest Metcalf, 1939-1940. Attorney.

Ronald V. Ware, 1940-1941. Tire dealer.

Willis H. "Bill" Hitt, 1941-1942. Soft drink dealer.

J.O. "Bob" Bowen, 1942-1943. Milk distributor.

Vincent Oaksmith, 1943-1944.

George McCampbell, 1944-1945. Teacher.

Stanley Peeler, 1945-1946. Auto dealer.

Willis H. "Bill" Hitt, 1946-1947.

E. Tinsley Halter, 1947-1948. Landscaping executive.

Lloyd C. Bell, 1948-1949. Electrical appliance dealer.

William P. Holland, 1949-1950. Barber.

L. Thomas Keating, 1950-1951. Marine hardware executive.

Houstin V. McMillan, 1951-1952. Journalist and radio executive.

H. Elmo Robinson, 1952-1953. Attorney.

Perry McCampbell, 1953-1954. Furniture merchant.

E.V. "Jack" Faircloth, 1954-1955. Truck firm dealer.

C. Harold Earnest, 1955-1956. Attorney.

Maurice E. "Buster" Holley, 1956-1957. Architect.

E.V. "Jack" Faircloth, 1957-1958.

Horace S. Miller, 1958-1959. News executive.

William P. Holland, 1959-1960.

Percy I. Hopkins, Jr., 1960-1962. Title firm operator.

C. Ben Holleman, 1962-1963. Insurance agent.

Bob Hawkey, 1963. Radio commentator.

Ray G. "Uncle Bim" Behm, 1963-1964. Lawn store operator.

Fred O. Easley, Jr., 1964-1966. Retired Air Force colonel.

C. Harold Earnest, 1966-1967.

Reid Moore, Jr., 1967-1968. Attorney.

David H. Brady, 1968-1969. Engineer.

Eugene W. Potter, 1969-1970. Real estate.

Fred O. Easley, Jr., 1970-1971.

Francis H. Foster, Jr. 1971-1972. Oil company representative.

Marvin Pope Anthony, 1972-1973. Retail executive.

Gilbert Ray Sparks, Jr., 1973-1974. Insurance.

Fred O. Easley, Jr., 1974-1975.

Richard E. Linn, 1975-1976. Insurance.

James M. Adams, 1976-1977. Attorney.

Marvin Pope Anthony, 1977-1978.

Helen Wilkes, 1978-1980. Retirement home operator.

James M. Adams, 1980-1981.

Michael D. Hyman, 1981-1982. Property manager.

Eva W. Mack, 1982-1984. School system supervisor.

Dwight Baber, 1984-1985. Architect.

Carol A. Roberts, 1985-1986. Homemaker.

Samuel A. Thomas, 1986-1987. Attorney.

Richard V. Reikenis, 1987-1988. Civil engineer.

Pat Pepper Schwab, 1988-1989. Marketing.

James O. Poole, 1989-1991. Pastor, teacher.

John F. "Jeff" Koons, 1991. Bottling executive.

Nancy M. Graham, 1991-1995. Attorney.

MAYOR NANCY GRAHAM ON CLEMATIS STREET, SUMMER 1994

Her vision of a downtown where people do more than work is still under construction, but the lawyer from Tennessee feels strongly that it will happen. "It's already happening. We get inquiries every day from good business people, developers of a quality we haven't had in a long time. It's going to take persistence — I prefer to say I'm persistent rather than stubborn. And I would not say we're there yet. But the momentum has started." Next pages: The modern skyline, 1994. ■

"During our centennial, we celebrate our past with a look at the future. We are at a critical point. To revive downtown, it's going to take commitment and persistence and about 10 years. But I know it's going to happen. We can be a great medium-size city, a major player in southeast Florida."

— West Palm Beach Mayor Nancy Graham, 1994

🌴

# Epilogue

## The Landmarks Today

When you drive around West Palm Beach and Palm Beach today, you pass pieces of history. This guide highlights many of the historic buildings mentioned in this book.

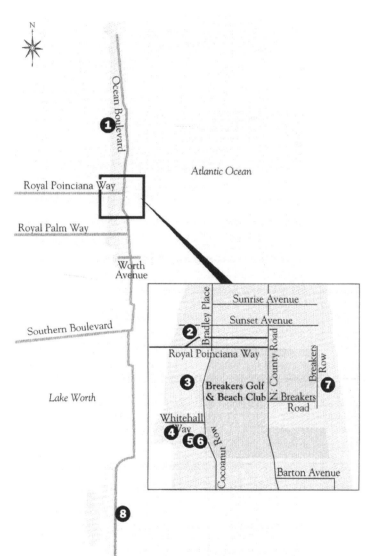

## In Palm Beach

**1** **Old Bethesda-by-the-Sea.** Built in 1894, the spired building can be seen from the bike trail on North Lake Way in Palm Beach (see old photograph, Page 15). It is now a private home. The current church building at Barton Road and South County Road was built in 1926.

*E.R. Bradley's Beach Club (foreground) in 1926; the Mediterranean revival style pavilion in back of the wood-frame Beach Club is what remains. Across the street is the railroad depot and the north wing of the Royal Poinciana Hotel.* ■

**2** **Last remnants of E.R. Bradley's home.** Col. E.R. Bradley's will stipulated that his famous Beach Club casino be razed and the property developed into a public park. Bradley died on Aug. 15, 1946. Today, an Oriental fireplace inset with antique mahjong tiles and a pavilion with fresco paintings along the walls remain in Bradley Park. They are the last remains of Bradley's home, which was adjacent to the casino.

*Aerial from early 1950s shows vacant land where the Royal Poinciana once stood.* ■

**3** **The slat house.** The only part of the Royal Poinciana Hotel still standing in its original spot, the domed slat house (greenhouse) was built to fill in part of the hotel damaged in the '28 hurricane. Today, office buildings and Dempsey's restaurant surround it.

**4** **Whitehall.** The marble palace Henry Flagler built for his third wife, Mary Lily Kenan, cost $2.5 million plus $1.5 million for furnishings in 1901. Today, Whitehall (above) is the Henry Morrison Flagler Museum.

**5** **Seagull Cottage.** The oldest house in Palm Beach, Seagull Cottage was built by Robert

McCormick of Denver in 1886. The house was included in Henry Flagler's 1893 land purchase (see Chapters 2 and 3), and Flagler lived there until Whitehall was built in 1901. The cottage was moved to the oceanfront north of The Breakers for use as a rental cottage, then moved back near its original site and restored in 1984.

**6** **Royal Poinciana Chapel.** Henry Flagler built the chapel in 1895 in exchange for land he needed for the hotels. The marriage of Cap Dimick's daughter, Belle, and Thomas Tipton Reese (see Chapter 3) was the first wedding at the chapel.

**7** **The Breakers.** Along with Whitehall, the twin-towered Breakers hotel is Flagler's most beautiful legacy. Built in 1926, it is the third Breakers (others were destroyed by fire in 1903 and 1925). The lobby is shown below.

**8** **First schoolhouse.** Dade County's first schoolhouse, built in 1886, was moved to Phipps Ocean Park in 1960. (Palm Beach was in Dade County before 1909.) It was rebuilt, so the pitch of the roof is noticeably different than the original (see Page 27).

# In West Palm Beach

*Compiled by William Dale Waters, the city's historic preservation planner*

**1** **First Church of Christ Scientist.** Built in 1928 in the Neo-Classical revival style.

**2** **The First Baptist Church.** Designed in a more modern Neo-Classical revival style. Built between 1959 and 1964.

**3** **The Norton Gallery of Art.** Designed by King and Wyeth of Palm Beach. Built in 1940 by Charles Trevail, the building is an excellent example of the Art Moderne style.

**4** **Woodlawn Cemetery entrance and the gatekeeper's cottage, 327 Acacia Road.** Cottage was built in 1905 in a Folk Victorian style (is is scheduled to be moved to the South Florida Fairgrounds). The cemetery gates (above) were designed by Harvey and Clarke and constructed in 1925.

**5** **Court Park, a potential historic district** (see Chapter 5). It includes the Mango Promenade, where all of the homes face this pedestrian path and are accessed from the rear by vehicles.

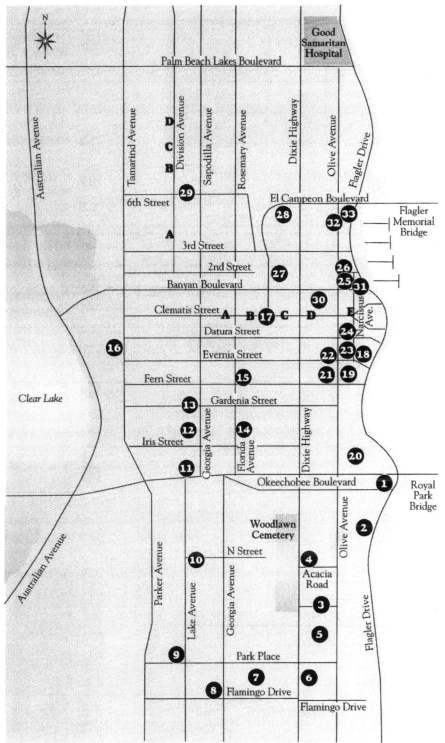

**6 Flamingo Park business district.**
1901 S. Dixie Highway. Lovett's Grocery
Store, built by C.J. Meerdink in 1937. Meerdink
was a prolific builder in West Palm Beach during
the Florida land boom and was responsible for the
Hotel Alma, which still stands at Florida Avenue
and Datura Street.

1905 S. Dixie Highway. The L.S. Nelson building built in 1928.

1910 S. Dixie Highway. A Mediterranean
revival structure built in 1925 by Arnold
Construction for commercial use.

1915-21 S. Dixie Highway. A Mediterranean
revival structure built in 1926 by E.B. Walton.
Walton was responsible for numerous structures
throughout the city and platted and developed the
Aravale and Arlington Place subdivisions.

**7 Flamingo Park.** See Chapter 5.

**8 The A.J. Comeau House, 701 Flamingo
Drive.** Designed by Harvey and Clarke and
constructed in 1924 in the Mediterranean revival
style by E.B. Walton. Comeau was responsible for
the landmark Comeau building on Clematis Street.

**9 The Armory Art Center, 1703 Lake Avenue**
(above). Designed by William Manly King in
the Art Deco style and built in 1939. It is in the
National Register of Historic Places.

**10 Grandview Heights** (see Chapter 5) and
**Howard Park.** Howard Park, which includes
the original turning basin for the stub canal, was
laid out in 1925 by the city's first superintendent of
streets and public improvements, D.D. Howard.

**11 Kravis Center for the Performing Arts.**

**12 Palm Beach High School/Twin Lakes High
School site.** Central School was designed by
W.W. Maughlin and built in 1908-09. The junior
high was built in 1915, and the old Palm Beach
High School (designed by William Manly King)
was built in 1922-23.

**13 Palm Beach Junior College building.**
Constructed in 1927 and designed by William
Manly King in the Mediterranean revival style.
Listed in the National Register of Historic Places.

**14 The First United Methodist Church and
Parsonage, 612 Florida Avenue.** Designed
by Spencer and Phillips and built by the Walker
Brothers in 1926.

**15 The Riddle House restoration.** The Karl
Riddle House, built in 1925 in Hillcrest, was
designed by Lester Geisler, who was an architect in
the firm of Addison Mizner. The house was moved
here from Hillcrest.

**16 The Seaboard Railroad passenger station**
(above). Designed by Harvey and Clarke in
the Mediterranean revival style in 1926. Listed in
the National Register of Historic Places.

*The 200 and 300 blocks of Clematis Street, looking west, in 1938.*

**17** **Clematis Street.**

**A.** West Palm Beach Police Station.

**B.** The 500 block, which includes Sewell's Hardware by John Volk and constructed by Chaulker and Lund in 1929, and the Flagler Court Hotel by the Blanchard Brothers.

**C.** The 300 block, which includes:

The Comeau building by Harvey and Clarke built in 1925 by Fred T. Lay and Co.

The Woolworth building, built in 1923 by Franklin G. Mason, with additions and modifications in the Art Deco style in 1932.

The Anthony building, built in 1919 by the Wilcox Brothers and designed by Van Allen.

The Harmonia Lodge, built by C.C. Haight in 1896.

The Farmers Bank and Trust Company (later the Diana Shops), built in 1913 with Mediterranean revival alterations in 1925 by Bruce Kitchell.

*Clematis and Olive, 1994: Hatch's department store (now the Galleria) is in the foreground at right; Farmers Bank building is at left (the front has been altered; see original on Page 120).* ◼

Hatch's Department Store, designed by John Volk in the Art Moderne style and constructed in 1936.

**D.** The 200 block, which includes:

The Palm Beach Mercantile building, built in 1916 and listed in the National Register of Historic Places.

The Citizens Bank building, built in 1923 and designed by G.L. Preacher.

**E.** The 100 block, which includes Fein's Department Store in the Art Moderne style and built in 1939.

**18** **Da Na Ra Arcade, 200-210 Datura Street** (southwest corner of Datura and Narcissus), now part of Fidelity Federal. Designed by Harvey and Clarke in 1925 and built by J.S. Wilson, this building has a twin on Palm Beach at Royal Palm Way and South County Road.

*Wagg building around 1926 (left) and today.*

**22** **The Wagg building, 215-217 S. Olive Avenue.** A Mediterranean revival office building designed by Harvey and Clarke in 1925 and built by J.S. Wilson, it served as the home of the Alfred H. Wagg Corp. Wagg developed much of West Palm Beach south of Southern Boulevard to the West Palm Beach canal, an area originally called Estates of South Palm Beach.

**19** **The Pennsylvania Hotel** (above, in the 1960s). Designed by Harvey and Clarke and completed by C.A.D. Bayley in 1925-26. Designed in the Mediterranean revival style, it is the last grand waterfront hotel in the city. Carmelite nuns, owners of the building, were planning to demolish it to build a high-rise nursing home in 1994.

**23** **The Harvey building.** Built by George W. Harvey, this was the city's tallest structure (14 floors) when completed in 1925.

**24** **The Harvey and Clarke block: The Guaranty building and the American National Bank building** (left). The Guaranty building, 120 S. Olive, was designed by Harvey and Clarke and built by Brown/Wilcox in 1922. The American National Bank (116 S. Olive) — the first structure in the city to be designed by Harvey and Clarke — was completed in 1921 by Brown/Wilcox. It is of the Neo-Classical style.

**20** **The Holy Trinity Episcopal Church.** Designed by Harvey and Clarke and constructed in 1923 by the Wilcox Brothers in the Spanish Colonial revival style.

**25** **The West Palm Beach City Hall.**

**26** **The St. Ann Catholic Church, rectory and parochial school.** Original church is a Neo-Gothic revival, wood-frame structure built in 1895 (original tower was damaged in the 1928 hurricane and removed in the 1940s). The rectory was built in 1903. The later church building is a Neo-Roman style with Norman influences.

**21** **The Central Farmer's Trust Company/The First Presbyterian Church, 301 S. Olive Avenue.** Built in 1925 by William Young and designed by Arthur L. Harmon, it was remodeled in 1934 and 1958.

**27** The Palm Beach County Governmental Center and courthouse, built in 1993-94, and — across the street and hidden from view — the original Palm Beach County courthouse, built in 1916. The 1916 courthouse was covered by an addition in 1969-70. A Save the Courthouse committee was working in 1994 to demolish the 1970 addition and save the original Neo-Classical style courthouse. The pillars from the courthouse now stand at the entrance to Hillcrest Memorial Park cemetery on Parker Avenue in West Palm Beach.

**28** The Florida State Board of Health Laboratory, 415 Fifth Street. Designed by Walker D. Willis and built by E.H. Barto in 1921 in the Neo-Classical revival style.

*The Palm Beach County courthouse (top, in a 1926 photo) was stripped of its columns (middle) and a modern addition was built around it in 1970 (bottom).* ■

Preston Tillman (left), founder of the Black Historical Preservation Society, his wife, Frankie, and the society board members outside the restored Gwen Cherry-Mollie Holt house in 1993. The house, headquarters of the society, once belonged to Holt, who was the grandmother of Gwen Cherry, the first black woman elected to the Florida Legislature. ▄

Payne Chapel.

**29** **The Northwest historic district** (see Chapter 5). Includes:

**A.** The Alice Frederick Mickens House, 801 Fourth Street. Constructed in 1917 for the prominent Mickens family (see Chapter 3).

**B.** The Mollie Holt-Gwen Cherry House, 625 Division Avenue. Designed in the Prairie style by the city's first black architect, Hazel Augustus, in 1925, the structure is now the home of the Palm Beach County Black Historical Society.

**C.** The Tabernacle Missionary Baptist Church, 801 Eighth Street. An unusual Romanesque revival structure built in 1925.

**D.** The Payne A.M.E. Chapel, 801 Ninth Street. Designed by Hazel Augustus, it is of the Gothic revival style and was built in 1924.

**30** **The W.D. Fagan building, 326 Banyan Boulevard (First Street).** An unusual arcaded structure designed in the Mediterranean revival style and built in 1925 by Harvey and Clarke.

**31** **The Helen Wilkes Hotel, previously known as the El Verano and the George Washington.** Designed in 1922, the original colonnaded Spanish Colonial revival structure has been significantly altered over the years.

**32** **The Dade County Bank Building.** Built in 1893 and floated over from Palm Beach to West Palm Beach in 1897. It stood at the northwest corner of Olive and Clematis, then it was moved to Myrtle Street, and then to its present location on Flagler Drive. It is now the Palm Beach High School Museum.

**33** **West Palm Beach Fishing Club.** Built in 1940 in the frame vernacular style.

✻

# Acknowledgments

---

## PIONEERS
## —IN—
## PARADISE

## The Staff

**Copy editor:** Louis Hillary Park

**Photo copy work:** Dave Barak, Hilary Carmichael, Gwyn Donahue

**Production coordinator:** Jay Ziglinski

**Color separations:** Jim Irvin, Alan Meismer, Dale Musial, Jacquelyn Waring

**Contributors:** Pat Crowley, Joel Engelhardt, Fred Schmidt and Ava Van de Water of *The Palm Beach Post*, writer Charlotte Maurer and photographer C.J. Walker

**Publishing coordinator:** Lynn Kalber

**Promotion and sales:** The Marketing, Circulation and Accounting departments of *The Palm Beach Post*

It has been our pleasure to work with some of the most giving, passionate historians and pioneers in Florida.

Our special thanks go to Susan Duncan and Dr. Nan Dennison of the Historical Society of Palm Beach County. We couldn't have done it without you.

We also owe a great debt to Darden Kettler Daves and Robin Wood of the West Palm Beach Centennial Committee. They have enough spark to fuel the city for another 100 years.

Dozens of other people helped us in our research and have our heartfelt thanks. They include:

Florida historians Donald Curl, Rodney Dillon, Bessie Wilson DuBois, Paul George, Howard Kleinberg, Stuart McIver and Jerald T. Milanich.

Jim Ponce, our favorite Flagler scholar.

William Dale Waters, historic preservation planner for West Palm Beach.

Joan Runkel, Tom Prestegard and Charles Simmons of the Henry Morrison Flagler Museum.

Karen Milano of the West Palm Beach Memorial Library, Florida Room.

The Black Historic Preservation Society, especially executive director Grace Barnett and Deborah Harris NDione.

David Willson for his pioneer research.

Michael Bornstein of the Save the Courthouse committee.

Pearl Messer Calloway for her Palm Beach High reunion book and her wonderful memories.

Bill Amason and Gary Robinson, West Palm Beach Police, and "Butch"

Barndt, West Palm Beach Fire Department.

Bobby Riggs and Reggie Stambaugh.

Mayor Nancy Graham.

James Waldeck II of Palm Beach County, who charted the city-limits maps.

Colin Rayner, founder of the Old Northwood Neighborhood Association.

Mary and Pete Brandenburg of El Cid.

Margie Yansura of Flamingo Park.

Patty and Rick High of Central Park.

Lory Volk of Prospect Park.

Dolores Brombacher and Steven Kettelle of Belair.

Laura Smith, Jay Sloane, Eileen Comiskey, Zada Rogerson and Kitty Carr Allison of Providencia Park.

The many readers who shared their personal memories with us.

And our pioneers — Inez Peppers Lovett, Tommy Reese and Alice Moore — whose conversations enhanced our lives.

We also would like to thank our families for their support — and for bringing us up with love and respect for South Florida, our home.

And, finally, we dedicate this book to Judge James R. Knott, who has preserved our city's colorful history for nearly 50 years. His "Brown Wrappers" — featuring lively memoirs of the early days — were a regular Sunday feature in *The Palm Beach Post* from 1978 to 1985. Thank you, Judge Knott. No one has told our stories so well — and with so much love.

— *JAN TUCKWOOD & ELIOT KLEINBERG*

## Charlotte Chapman Maurer,
*author of Chapter 7*

*Charlotte Maurer in front of her family's house on Greymon Drive, 1992.* ■

Charlotte Chapman knew she wanted to be a writer even before Mrs. Hiatt drilled her in grammar at Conniston Junior High. After college and World War II, she worked at *The New Yorker*, then married and raised a family. Her father, J. Leo Chapman, practiced law in West Palm Beach for 60 years. He lived in their house on Greymon Drive until his death at age 101 in 1991. Vera Chapman died in 1958 and Charlotte's younger sister, Fay, died in 1992.

Charlotte would like to thank the following people who shared their memories with her: Gloria Steed Hunter, Jackie Mosler Kuntz, Nancy Riddle Madden, Alma Lu Meerdink and Harold Merry.

Charlotte now lives in Maine, but West Palm Beach is still first in her heart.

# Picture Credits

The Historical Society of Palm Beach County provided most of the historic photographs in this book, and the modern photography was done by E.A. Kennedy III of *The Palm Beach Post*, unless noted here.

Dust jacket, cover: Courtesy of Darden Kettler Daves.

Back: Top, George Panos postcard collection. Bottom, Sherman Zent, *The Palm Beach Post*.

Page 7: Courtesy of Edward M. Sears.

### Chapter 1

Page 10: Map courtesy of George Panos.

### Chapter 2

Page 12: Courtesy of David Willson.
Pages 14, 16, 17: Sketches courtesy of David Willson.
Page 18: Courtesy of David Willson.
Pages 20, 22, 23: Courtesy of David Willson.

### Chapter 3

Page 29, 32, 33: Photos courtesy of the Henry Morrison Flagler Museum.
Pages 34, 35: George Panos postcard collection.
Page 46: C.J. Walker, *The Palm Beach Post*.
Pages 48, 49: Courtesy of the Henry Morrison Flagler Museum.
Pages 53, 55: Courtesy of T.T. Reese Jr.
Page 60: George Panos postcard collection.
Pages 62, 63, 64: Courtesy of Alice Moore.
Page 68: Courtesy of William Sned.
Page 72: Courtesy of Sandra Sheen McCall.
Page 73: Courtesy of Sarah Gates Carroll.

Page 74: *Palm Beach Post* file photo.
Page 75: George Panos postcard collection.
Page 77: Courtesy of the Henry Morrison Flagler Museum.
Page 78: Small photo, courtesy of Sandra Sheen McCall.
Page 86: Small photo, courtesy of Darden Kettler Daves.
Page 91: Courtesy of Ineria Hudnell and Bettye Dawson.
Page 92: Walter Walker Collection, Black Historical Preservation Society.

### Chapter 6

Pages 124-125: *Palm Beach Post* file photos.

### Chapter 7

Courtesy of Charlotte Chapman Maurer.

### Chapter 8

Page 140: Collage photographed by Mark Mirko, *The Palm Beach Post*.
Page 141: Courtesy of Lucy Seader; collage photographed by Dave Barak.
Page 142: Small photo, courtesy of Dr. Reginald Stambaugh.
Page 144: Courtesy of Kay Hutchins.
Pages 146-147: Courtesy of the subjects.

### Chapter 9

Page 151: *Palm Beach Post* file photos;
Page 160-161: Courtesy of Jon Stoll and the Carefree Theater and the Myers family.
Page 162: Norton Gallery photograph from *Palm Beach Post* files.
Page 163: *Palm Beach Post* files.
Page 165: Small photo, *Palm Beach Post* files.
Page 167: Courtesy of Caroline Browning
Page 168: Courtesy of Bettye Dawson.

Page 169: *Palm Beach Post* files.
Page 170: Courtesy of Buck Kinnaird.
Page 171: Courtesy of WPTV-Channel 5 and Lynn Kalber.
Page 172: Courtesy of WPTV-Channel 5 and *Palm Beach Post* files.
Pages 173-175: *Palm Beach Post* files.
Pages 176-177: Courtesy of the subjects.

### Chapter 10

Pages 180-181: *Palm Beach Post* files (except airport photograph).
Pages 183: Brochure courtesy of the West Palm Beach Centennial Committee.
Page 184: Auditorium, *Palm Beach Post* files.
Page 185: *Palm Beach Post* files.
Page 186: Burdines, *Palm Beach Post* files.
Pages 187-189: *Palm Beach Post* files.
Pages 191-193: *Palm Beach Post* files.

### Chapter 11

Pages 194-195: C.J. Walker, *The Palm Beach Post*.
Pages 196-197: *Palm Beach Post* files.
Page 198: Greg Lovett, *The Palm Beach Post*.
Page 199: Loren G. Hosack and Allen Eyestone, *The Palm Beach Post*.
Pages 200-201: C.J. Walker.
Page 202-203: Drawings courtesy Team Plan Inc.
Page 205: Mark Mirko, *The Palm Beach Post*.

### Chapter 12

Page 210: Whitehall, C.J. Walker; The Breakers, Mark Mirko, *The Palm Beach Post*.
Page 212: Seaboard Station, C.J. Walker, *The Palm Beach Post*.
Page 215: *Palm Beach Post* files.
Page 216: C.J. Walker, *The Palm Beach Post*.

# Bibliography

*Boone's Florida Historical Markers and Sites*, by Floyd E. Boone
*Centennial History of the West Palm Beach Fire Department*, by Ron Johnson
*The Enterprise of Florida: Pedro Menéndez de Avilés and the Spanish Conquest of 1565-1568*, by Eugene Lyons
*The Fire History of the City of West Palm Beach*, by B.T. Kennedy
*First Encounters: Spanish Explorations in the Caribbean and the United States*, Edited by Jerald T. Milanich and Susan Milbrath
*Florida Almanac*, by Del Marth and Martha J. Marth
*The Florida Handbook*, by Allen Morris
*Florida from Indian Trail to Space Age*, by Charlton W. Tebeau and Ruby Leach Carson
*Florida's Past: People and Events that Shaped the State*, Volumes 1-3, by Gene M. Burnett
*Florida, A Short History*, by Dr. Michael Gannon
*Funk & Wagnalls Standard Reference Encyclopedia*
*Glimpses of South Florida History*, by Stuart McIver
*A History of Florida*, by Charlton W. Tebeau

*Flagler, Rockefeller Partner and Land Baron*, by Edward N. Akin
*Florida's Flagler*, by Sidney Walter Martin
*History of Juno Beach, History of Jupiter Lighthouse, Shipwrecks in Jupiter Inlet, History of the Loxahatchee River*, all by Bessie Wilson DuBois
*History of the Second Seminole War, 1835-1842*, by John K. Mahon
*History of the West Palm Beach Police Centennial History and Yearbook*, by Bill Amason and Gary Robinson
*Early Lantana, Her Neighbors and More*, by Mary Collar Linehan
*The Notorious Ashley Gang*, by Hix C. Stuart
*Palm Beach: A Century of Heritage*, by Wilma Bell Spencer
*Palm Beach County: An Illustrated History*, by Donald Curl
*Pioneer Life in Southeast Florida*, by Charles W. Pierce
*Public Faces — Private Lives*, by Karen Davis
*Yesterday's Palm Beach*, by Stuart McIver
The archives of *The Palm Beach Post, The Palm Beach Times, The Palm Beach Daily News* and *The Tropical Sun*
The Florida and South Florida historical societies and the archives of the state of Florida

# Index

*West Palm Beach City Park, 1930s.*

Florida Tourists.